All for Love

Also in the Contents series

Catch the Moon   SUE WELFORD
In Between *edited by* MIRIAM HODGSON
Listen to the Dark   MAEVE HENRY
Midwinter   MAEVE HENRY
The Spark Gap   JULIE BERTAGNA
throwaways   IAN STRACHAN
Time Wreck   VIVIEN ALCOCK
The Vision   PETE JOHNSON
A Winter Night's Dream   ANDREW MATTHEWS
The Wormholers   JAMILA GAVIN

Contents

All for Love

edited by Miriam Hodgson

First published in Great Britain in 1997 by Mammoth
an imprint of Reed International Books Ltd
Michelin House, 81 Fulham Road, London SW3 6RB
and Auckland, Melbourne, Singapore and Toronto

You Are Very Beautiful © 1997 Keith Gray
Act of Love © 1997 Theresa Breslin
Words Last For Ever © 1997 Malorie Blackman
Just Friends © 1997 Jamila Gavin
Letter from Kalymnos © 1997 Michael Morpurgo
The House that Darren Built © 1997 Carlo Gébler
The Fate Formula © 1997 Elizabeth Arnold
All for Love © 1997 Jenny Koralek

This volume copyright © 1997 Mammoth

The authors have asserted their moral rights in accordance with
the Copyright, Designs and Patents Act 1988

ISBN 0 7497 2920 1

10 9 8 7 6 5 4 3 2 1

A CIP catalogue record for this book is available
from the British Library

Printed and bound in Great Britain
by Cox & Wyman Ltd, Reading, Berkshire

This paperback is sold subject to the condition
that it shall not, by way of trade or otherwise,
be lent, resold, hired out, or otherwise circulated
without the publisher's prior consent in any form
of binding or cover other than that in which
it is published and without a similar condition
including this condition being imposed
on the subsequent purchaser.

Contents

You Are Very Beautiful **Keith Gray**	1
Act of Love **Theresa Breslin**	14
Words Last For Ever **Malorie Blackman**	23
Just Friends **Jamila Gavin**	36
Letter from Kalymnos **Michael Morpurgo**	50
The House that Darren Built **Carlo Gébler**	62
The Fate Formula **Elizabeth Arnold**	80
All for Love **Jenny Koralek**	93

You Are Very Beautiful

Keith Gray

Susan wouldn't let me kiss her goodbye so I wouldn't let her follow me into the train station. I stuffed the earplugs from my Walkman into my ears and wrapped my coat tightly round myself. I hunched up on the cold, plastic seat in the glass bubble of the waiting-room. If I'd needed any definite proof that there was nothing left to be salvaged, if I'd needed reassurance that it was over completely between us now, then I sure as hell had got it.

Newcastle station was busy that day. The platforms filled and cleared, the announcer's metallic voice rang around the high hangar-like walls, the trains stopped only briefly. I had over ten minutes to wait and kept a close eye on the footbridge which spanned the tracks, scanning the bustling faces for one that might look a little like Susan's. Or a lot like Susan's. Maybe.

Some had her blonde hair, but not the way she wore it. Some had her pale skin, but not the rosiness in her cheeks. I wondered if any had her smile. Or if they had eyes which watered whenever they were overcome by giggles. If any of them knew all the words to *Les Miserables* . . .

I turned the volume up on my Walkman. I clutched my coat tighter still. I didn't want any of the outside world getting in at me. I stared at my feet and waited for my train. This was killing me. It was such a hopeless feeling. Such a hopeless, frustrating feeling. I couldn't believe that something which had ruled my life for so long was now at such a definite end. If our relationship had been a hamster then at least I could have buried it in the back garden and said, well, he had a happy life. We did our best for him . . . But I couldn't seem to do anything about this situation. There quite simply didn't seem to be any way to make myself feel any better.

A mother and her daughter joined me in the waiting-room on platform 4. The daughter was about my age, about sixteen, a mass of dark, curly hair hanging straggly to her shoulders, but she didn't look at me. The mother was ageing, grey, and wouldn't look at me either. I don't think they even noticed I was there. I surreptitiously turned down

You Are Very Beautiful

the volume on my Walkman and tuned into their conversation. It was about having to change at Darlington, not about me.

I realised I had a problem with this. I realised I wanted them to notice me. I coughed gently and fidgeted on the bum-curved plastic of the waiting-room seat. I made an elaborate show of swapping the cassette in my Walkman; fumbling in my bag for something I wanted to listen to, winding the tape to the very end with a pencil, snapping the little stereo's door shut with a sharp clap. Then fidgeted some more, but was still awarded with little more than a cursory glance.

Susan used to notice me. Used to. Before she'd moved up here to Newcastle. We'd been going out for almost a year, if you included the last four months since she'd moved. Almost a year, but not quite. Next month it'd be a year. Or would've been a year... I'd already bought her an anniversary card. I'd already written in it.

My mum had warned me about this. She'd told me that Susan was going to meet new people, make new friends. Of course I hadn't believed her. But then the letters had got further and further apart, the waiting in between them longer and longer, and the invites to come up and stay had been put back and rain-checked and squirmed out of. And now I hated my mother for being so bloody all-knowing and prophetic. And I knew exactly what she was going to say, oh yes. About fish in the sea. About only being young. About having plenty more time for this sort of thing just yet. But none of it would help. No way. Not at all. Because I also remembered something else she had once told me.

I could have only been about seven when she'd said it. But I'd remembered it. It had stuck in my mind all this time. I'd asked her why she and Dad had got married and I think she'd taken quite a bit of pleasure in telling me some old stories from her youth. I guess she'd thought a lot of what she said would go over my head and I guess most of it had. But she'd said that she'd found her someone, her ideal partner in my father, and that was why she'd married him. She'd said she truly believed that everyone had an ideal partner in the world somewhere, everyone had a someone. And I'd never forgotten that.

In fact it was the memory right at the very top of the pile, brightly lit and neon even, as the train that would take me home and away from Susan pulled up at platform 4, and the girl and her mother hurried out of the waiting-room without a glance at me.

Hey, Mum, maybe I'd found my someone. Maybe no one else is going to notice me. Maybe I just lost my someone. Maybe we only ever get one shot at this someone business and I've just blown it big time. Ever thought of that? Ever considered that might happen? Have you?

I joined the crowd on the cold platform. I fought briefly with the hustle and bustle, long enough to see if Susan had come to say goodbye after all, and was then jostled on to the train, disappointed

You Are Very Beautiful

but not surprised. I didn't really care where I sat and let the flow carry me to the nearest available seat. I didn't notice the little reserved ticket sticking out of it. I pushed my bag into the rack above my head and slumped down. I was sitting at a table, the two facing seats and the one next to me were empty. I hoped they'd stay that way until I changed at Doncaster. I shuffled over into the next seat, the aisle seat, to try and help keep it that way.

I had brought a book with me to read and took it out. It wasn't very exciting, I'd got bored with it on the journey coming up here, but it was a good excuse to ignore the other passengers, just like they were ignoring me. They all squeezed by down the narrow aisle, scraping me with their coats and bags. None of them stopped to sit at my table. None of them seemed to notice me. I noticed people, so why couldn't they notice me?

I made a sudden point of noticing the people around me. The business woman looking for a seat; tall, briefcase and glasses, dark suit. The two lads who looked like students slouching in the seats behind me; one goatee beard, one Nirvana T-shirt, two rucksacks. The pretty girl sitting at the table opposite mine on the other side of the aisle; long, fair ponytail and freckles, pale sweater, book open in her hands much like me, not really reading it much like me, looking at . . . me.

I dropped my eyes.

I pretended to read my book for a bit. And just as the train was beginning to trundle its way out of the station I glanced up again, and sure enough she wasn't looking at me any more. So I looked at her instead.

The senior conductor was telling us all about the buffet car and the different stops along the Intercity's route, but I didn't think she was listening. She wasn't really reading her book either. She rested her head back against the seat to catch the warmth of the sun through the window. Her skin seemed to shine, the radiance highlighting the spray of delicate hair across her face. Her eyebrows were long and slim, her eyes almost feline-looking. She was watching the Tyne as it passed beneath us. I made a guess. Seventeen? Eighteen? Maybe as old as twenty. Definitely older than me. She was silhouetted for a brief moment as the train turned with the track and the sun was in my eyes. She had a small, straight nose, a strong jaw.

She kind of reminded me of Susan. Not much. But enough. Enough to keep me stealing glances all the way to Durham. And she caught me. I tried to pretend I was staring past her, looking out of the window at the fields and trees, but just wasn't able to drop my eyes in time. Not that she seemed to mind.

She smiled at me.

I couldn't believe it. This pretty girl . . . This beautiful woman had smiled at me. I smiled back of course, although I think it looked a bit

You Are Very Beautiful

goofy. I was embarrassed, I wasn't expecting it. She'd caught me off guard. I turned to watch the countryside scenery flash by my window.

Our train stopped at Durham to gather some more passengers from a new platform. An elderly lady with a bag almost twice her size insisted on sitting next to me. I couldn't understand why, until I noticed the reservation tickets poking out of the top of the seats. I then felt obliged to help her fight with her luggage, hefting it up and into the high racking. It was a struggle; she kept on calling me a wonderful young man and a credit to my mother, and I actually had to stand on my seat to push the bag home. But even then it hung rather precariously over the rack's edge.

I was blushing furiously. I knew the rest of the passengers had been watching our little performance, cabaret on the 125, and of course I included the girl across the aisle in that list of passengers. I settled awkwardly back into my seat and dared a glance across at her. And this time I caught her watching me. She smiled at me again. A little raised-eyebrow smile. A shared, young persons' smile at the expense of adults everywhere.

The train continued its journey south, next stop Darlington. I knew I'd stolen somebody's seat but I didn't want to move, not now. Not while I had the chance of winning another smile. I may have been being greedy, I'd already had two, but I told myself that surely a third wasn't too much to ask. I wondered if I dared to step across the aisle to sit with her. I wondered if I dared to speak with her. I tried to tell myself it wouldn't be such a ridiculous thing to do. I told myself that people lost dozens of friends every day because they didn't have the guts to talk with strangers.

The elderly lady next to me started up a conversation then. She was all home-perm and wasted Oil of Ulay. She was telling me about how she was on her way to visit her daughter at Bristol University. I only listened with the ear nearest to her. But I wanted to seem polite. I put in the odd nod and 'um' and 'yes' where I thought one was needed. Old women always seemed to want to talk to me on trains or at bus stops, I think I must have had one of those faces. So I listened to her monologue, although really I was trying to watch the girl across the aisle, whilst pretending to read my book. It wasn't easy, but I seemed to be managing.

I wasn't sure whether or not she was actually reading her book either. Her eyes were certainly fixed on the pages, and she flipped them at honest intervals, but I was nurturing a fantasy that maybe she was stealing glimpses of me as well. I doubted it, of course. I didn't truly believe it. I knew Susan was the only girl who had ever bothered herself with giving me a second glance. And this girl certainly wasn't Susan. I'd left Susan in Newcastle. Or rather Susan had left me by moving to Newcastle.

The closer we drew to Darlington the more anxious I became about having stolen somebody's seat. I made sure my bag was in easy reach as the train pulled into the station. A dark-haired lad of about my age came to sit at the table. He sat down opposite the elderly woman and stared out of the window. He was lucky, he'd had the foresight not to take off his headphones. It was no use the woman telling him about her daughter's adventures in Bristol. I wished I'd been wearing my own earplugs when she'd sat herself next to me.

A second woman joined us at our table, sitting in the seat facing me. She was quite different from the lady next to me, not quite as round; sharper with her neat, short hair and long, straight face, but the two of them dived immediately into conversation. I didn't join in, even though I secretly agreed the weather had been terrible recently. This second lady had taken the last available seat. Or rather the second to last. I sneaked a peek at the long, thin reservation ticket sticking out of the top of my chair. The typed bold letters read YORK. And York was the next stop along the Intercity's route.

In between Darlington and York I tried to take in as much of the pretty girl from across the aisle as I possibly could. I watched her undo and then re-pull her hair into its long ponytail. I watched her unconsciously stroke her cheek as she read, and I made a vow to someday read that book too. All three of the seats round her table were still empty, I knew I could easily have stepped across that aisle between us and joined her. But I didn't. I wouldn't. She'd been polite to me, that was all.

The senior conductor announced York and I reluctantly got to my feet. I was loath to leave my stolen seat, feeling like I was leaving yet another beautiful girl behind. I apologised as I reached across the woman next to me and retrieved my bag from above her head. I fumbled with it, feeling that everybody must think I was some terrible seat thief, the committer of the most heinous of passenger crimes. I mumbled in an embarrassed kind of way about this not really being my seat. I reckon I was blushing again. I caught myself apologising for my unruly behaviour that little bit too loudly and hurried away up the aisle towards the next car.

She'd been watching me, and listening too. And as I'd scurried away she'd given me that third smile I'd been after. It had been sympathetic, as if she wanted me to know that she knew my position all too well herself.

The next car along was the buffet car. I found myself a corner and leaned in it, not wanting the same problem with another seat elsewhere. The train pulled itself carriage by carriage away from York station. Not long now before Doncaster. The next stop. My stop. I took out my book again and continued to pretend to read it. I was only pretending because basically the words didn't mean that much to me.

You Are Very Beautiful

Not after winning a third smile. Maybe, I thought, just maybe I wasn't being greedy after all.

I looked up from my book to see the girl from across the aisle standing in front of me. She smiled at me as she swayed slightly with the motion of the train. She was taller than me. A man with his shirt sleeves rolled up past his elbows squeezed by her with his coffee and cheeseburger. The aroma from the food was no match for this girl's perfume. 'Your seat's still free. It's not been taken. Nobody got on at York,' she told me.

I didn't know where to look. I tried my book, but that was no good. I would have taken a step back if I hadn't already been leaning against the wall. I offered her a weak smile and a shrug. 'That's OK. Mine's the next stop anyway,' I mumbled. The heat of a blush was in my face for the third time that day. But when she smiled at me again I realised that I hadn't blushed quite as many times at her as she'd smiled at me.

And I kicked myself when she walked away back to her seat. I didn't even bother pretending to read my book any more. I paced back and forth, up and down the buffet car. Doncaster was coming. I'd change there to go home, back to my mother who probably already had her speech prepared. She may have even practised it, refined a few details here and there. But I still knew I wouldn't want to hear it. It was just that my reasons why not had changed now.

Did I have the guts to go to this girl and say thank you? Did she already know what wonders her smile could perform? To be ignored by the mother and daughter in the draughty waiting-room of platform 4 was one thing, to be acknowledged by this girl's smile was surely another. Outside the train the fields quickly gave way to scattered houses. I had to do something, I couldn't let this pass me by. The train burst through the outskirts of Doncaster. Susan wasn't forgotten, never would be, she was simply buried under the rose bush next to the hamster I'd had when I'd been at junior school.

The senior conductor was thanking me for travelling with him all the way to Doncaster when I borrowed a pen from the attendant in the buffet car. The platform slid slowly into place as I scribbled on the inside back cover of my book. I hoped the author wouldn't mind.

I stepped out on to the platform. I'd been lucky, it was on the right side. My heart was thumping in my chest, my book was pressed hard against it. I felt a little light-headed as I approached the window and tapped lightly on the glass.

The girl from across the aisle, who was now on the other side of the window, looked at me. The passengers sitting around her, the two ladies and the boy I shared a table with all looked at me. The crowd on the platform stopped briefly in their tracks to see what was happening. The whole world was watching me.

My hand shook slightly as I bent back the cover of my book. I dropped my bag to the ground so that I could hold it up to the window with both hands. I saw the girl's eyes flick to the message I'd written in big, bold capital letters. The train cheered me as it started to move, its engine hailing me in its eagerness to carry this girl wherever she wanted to go. I saw her smile, so much bigger than my letters. And again her eyes flicked to what I'd written as the train moved away, turning her head to read it three times, four times, to make sure what she was seeing was really there: YOU ARE VERY BEAUTIFUL.

And it was. Because she was.

Act of Love
Theresa Breslin

The trick, as Captain John Ainsley had discovered, was in how you placed the bullet. Too close, and the skull exploded, smearing one's uniform with gore and brain tissue. Too far back, and the deed was left incomplete, with the man on the ground gazing up at you with the eyes of a kitten awaiting drowning.

Once, a starlight shell had burst around him as he had made just such a mistake, and the soldier he was crouched beside in no-man's-land, an older man, had looked up at him, smiled, and said, 'You'll have to try again, son.'

He had returned from that sortie trembling, rushing to the brandy flask in the support trench, gabbling what had happened. His CO had

Act of Love

taken him aside and spoken to him firmly, explaining yet again that what he did was for the best.

'Get a grip, man. Those casualties left lingering out there for the rats to eat alive, or hanging on the barbed-wire night after night, would curse you for not doing it.'

He had protested, declaring it inhuman. A hateful thing to do.

'Actually,' replied the CO, 'I consider it an act of love.'

It rarely happened now that he got the shakes. He had become an expert at dispatching a man with a single bullet, and avoiding a mess to clean up later. He took the identity disc from the dead private's neck, and put his pistol back in the leather holster on his belt. His fingers scarcely trembled, despite the fact that the boy he had just killed could have been no more than fifteen years old. Ten years younger than himself . . . a child . . . whereas he, after four months of this war without sense, was an old man.

He crawled back to the other soldier who might yet live and began to help him drag himself towards their forward trenches. They moved cautiously, yet in the knowledge of the gentleman's agreement regarding collecting casualties and parapet repairs at night. Enemy action was suspended to allow both sides to retrieve their wounded and get them back down the supply roads in the shadow of darkness.

Each week Captain Ainsley wrote home in pages torn from his field diary, but nothing he wrote described what he saw each day. The stench of the dead and dying pervading each place. Their defences, as the line moved forward and they gained two hundred yards, were built on top of the bodies of the German dead. And no doubt when they were driven back three weeks later, he supposed the Boche used the British corpses for the same end. Should he be surprised when his mother sent him packages of mint tea and bath salts, when he needed carbolic soap and dry matches?

Fleas jumped everywhere, and lice lay in the seams of your clothes. Insolent bluebottles, swollen so large as to be cumbersome in flight, buzzed round your head, and rats, which you were not allowed to shoot, crawled blood-bloated and rabid among the dead. The vile side of nature triumphant and the sweetness crushed. No birdsong, no flowers, nor plants nor perfumed air.

When he first happened upon Private Sam Hinslewood, chatting with his friends and playing softly on his mouth organ, John Ainsley stopped to listen. And then was drawn back, evening after evening to the same company, standing to the rear of the group as Sam read out his letters from home. There was his wife, Mary, trying to manage the farm on her own. They had a boy, Adam, rising ten. Sam described the seasons as they fell. The year was on the turn. The shire horses would be put to the plough, Tom and Colt, turning the earth, preparing the land to receive the seed.

The man had a gift. He was a natural born storyteller. The words, as he said them, came alive. One could hear the peewits in the meadow, see the pale golden ears of barley ripen as he spoke.

On one occasion they had noticed him, and as the soldiers scrambled to their feet and saluted, Captain Ainsley made a small sign with his hand.

'Compliments need not be paid on active service.'

He recited the words from the staff manual and moved away, strangely embarrassed at having been discovered.

He had spent his evenings reading at first, then drinking more and more, and always, always, compiling the casualty lists. He never mentioned this in his letters home. His parents wrote back in fulsome praise of his rapid promotion to the rank of Captain. The bridge club had been very impressed. He neglected to inform them that the promotion was automatic and depended on the death of one's superior officer. He made a grim smile when his father had written to say he was now reaping the benefit of the officer training, which he knew he had hated. Captain Ainsley reflected that learning to pass the port to the left did not seem significantly relevant at the moment. It became much more important to know how Sam's boy was progressing. In the daily letters which his wife wrote she described the lad, ruddy and sturdy-legged playing in the fields around their farm. Her love, and the child's, moved among them all.

Once, when they had been shifted along the line, they had halted for rest at a crossroads. Under the trees, outside an estaminet, Sam and his friends had gathered. And the Captain with the rest had laughed out loud at one of his stories. All the men had turned to the sound of the stranger amongst them, and he caught Sam's eye, flushed, and walked away quickly.

He found that he was not as happy in the company of his fellow officers. Yes, a shared cigarette under the rain cape, tears of rain dripping from the low eaves of the farmhouses. And the anxious drinking together as they discussed home and troops and the British High Command. But it wasn't the same. Under the roar of the guns, the heavy bombardment that now came day after day, and the chatter of the machine-gun fire he knew where he wanted to be, who he needed to be with.

And if it came to it, as it would, when they went over the top, up the short wooden ladder, whistles screaming, he prayed that he would not fail them. In the choking gas, and the smoke, eyes streaming, as they had done in the smoke in the railway station where she had come to bid him farewell, her eyes sliding away, her attention caught by movement beyond him.

'Oh, George, look!' she cried, laying a gloved hand on his father's arm. 'A military band! I do love a brass band!' And she had walked forward to see the parade.

His father, for once aware of his sensitivities, said, 'You musn't mind your mother so much. Women are always taken with such things.'

His father had shaken his hand firmly and he had saluted and boarded the train.

The smoke still drifted; here and there, each evening, as he searched among the bodies. And as he slithered on his belly now in the sucking mud, hoping for one to bring back, he came suddenly upon a huge rat. Rolling to one side to avoid it, he felt the hard metal of a land-mine under him.

It exploded with a crash which knocked him senseless and hurled him into the air yards away. When he opened his eyes at last, he knew that it was the same night, and that he could not even lift his head.

'What's amiss?' Sam's voice spoke in his ear.

'Arms, legs... can't move them,' Ainsley said. And his voice, when he heard it, filled him with contempt for himself. Pathetic and weak.

Sam tried to assess the damage. His hands, searching across the uniform, touched the caved-in breastbone, felt the shattered limbs. The Captain was in great pain, his jaw clenched lest a sound escape. Sam calculated: twenty minutes or so to drag him the few short yards to the trench, the wait for the stretcher-bearers to take him to the reserve post, another twenty minutes to the nearest field dressing station, no morphine, no doctor. Hours on the jolting horse-drawn ambulance cart to get him back down the line. It would be at least a day before the Captain got any relief.

'Leave me. Go back.'

'Uhuh,' the older man grunted.

'Let me raise you up here.' He slid his hand under the tunic collar at the back of Ainsley's neck. The Captain whimpered as he touched him.

As Sam's fingers sank into the soft porridge of the remains of John Ainsley's skull, a magnesium flare lit up the sky above, and he could see the man's face illuminated in the glow. The Captain's eyes were dull, the light fading. His face tallow-candle yellow.

'Go back,' Ainsley said again. 'I order you to.'

'No, no, man,' Sam soothed him. 'Hush. Hush.'

There was a rattle of fire along the line. Sam cursed. Some silly beggar. There had been word of troop changes on the German side a few days ago. A nervous new recruit must have loosed off a few rounds.

'Hey!' came a shout from his own side. 'Let up, Fritz. We want some shut-eye over here.'

'Sweet dreams, Tommy,' a voice called back. '*Gute Nacht.*'

'Go back,' the Captain whispered to Sam. 'The men need you.'

'You're the officer,' said Sam. 'It's you they need.'

'You give them hope.'

'And you give them courage,' replied Sam. 'They'd follow you to hell.'

'They have. We are in hell.'

There was silence between them. Sam's arm lay still round the other man's neck.

'We'll wait a bit,' he said, 'until it's quieter, and then see if we can get back.'

'Tell me about your boy,' whispered the Captain.

'My boy?' Sam repeated.

'The lad, Adam. The farm . . . your wife, Mary . . . the horses . . . your life.'

'Oh,' said Sam. 'It's very ordinary. Hard work. Up at sunup, work 'til sundown. But the countryside is beautiful. Mary collects berries, makes jam, it's peaceful . . . so peaceful . . .' He stopped, he hesitated. 'This is what you want to hear?'

Captain Ainsley nodded.

So Sam talked on, describing their way of life, the crops, from seeding to harvest, the animals, and the flowers in the hedgerows.

'You have the gift of storytelling,' said the Captain. 'I have the very smell of gardenia in my head. It is my mother's favourite perfume . . . I remember she used to come and kiss me each evening after Nanny had tucked me up in bed. She would be dressed in a pretty dress, always such a pretty dress . . . I wanted her to wait to hug me . . .'

He stopped then, recalling the night when he had clung on, sobbing childish sobs, begging her to stay, and she had pushed him back against his pillows, complaining he had crushed her frock. At that moment his father had come into the room. They were already late for the theatre, he said. Did she have to kiss the boy still? He was too old now for that. She would make him soft. And his father had blown out the night-light, and he was left in the dark.

He looked about him with a start. It was dark now, a strange closing darkness that was advancing towards him. He began to shake as he had done that night.

'Hug me,' he cried. 'For the love of God, comfort me.'

Sam gathered the boy to him and held him close against his chest. And stroked his face and told him more of his son and his farm.

The stars were fading. Sam looked to the sky in the east, louring and ominous with dark cloud. He knew he must move, but he kept talking, although he was aware that the Captain was barely conscious. It seemed to him that the boy was merging with the landscape, grey face, grey sky, grey bones, becoming as one with the surrounding glutinous mud.

So then Sam, without withdrawing his arm from under his Captain's neck, and still speaking quietly as if to gentle a skittish mare, reached with his free hand to slide the muzzle of the pistol into position beside John Ainsley's head.

Words Last For Ever

Malorie Blackman

Dear Robert,

I'm really sorry about doing it this way, but every time I try to talk to you, I just don't seem to be able to get the words out. That's why I finally plumped for this letter – which is something I always swore I'd never, ever do. But I had to. You see, the trouble is, I feel things too deeply. I always have done. That's why it's so hard for me to say no or to hurt someone. And I don't want to hurt you – God knows I don't. I like you. I really do.

It's just that, I don't want to go out with you any more. There, I've said it. I want you to know, I really do like you and I hope we can still be friends. I'd hate to lose your friendship. But I do feel it would be better if we stopped going out. It would solve all kinds of problems – for both of us. Don't you agree? Please don't think I'm being cowardly about this. I'm not. But you and I together, it causes so many – what's the word I'm looking for? – complications.

Take last Saturday, for instance. An ordinary, every day trip to the cinema turned into . . . well, turned into an ordeal. I'd be lying if I said otherwise. We were stared and pointed at and I heard the people in the queue behind us making really nasty comments. I know you said we should just ignore them, and I did try – but I couldn't.

Words hurt. It's that simple.

Words stick and implant themselves and become part of you as physical pain never can. The pain from a punch or a slap fades and disappears eventually. Words last for ever. I'm not putting this very well. Robert, I guess what I'm trying to say is, I'm just not used to it. I thought I could handle all the attention the two of us together would provoke, but yesterday evening was the final straw. Now I realise that I was just lying to myself and being unfair to you.

I'm sure that once you've had a chance to sit down and think about it, you'll see I'm right.

So take care of yourself and I wish you only good things.

                        Yours in friendship,

                        Penny

Words Last For Ever

Dear Penny,

This is the third letter I've written to you. I had to tear up the other two as soon as I'd finished them before the words burnt through the paper they were written on. If you want to stop going out with me because you've gone off me or because I have a bad case of body odour or swamp breath, then that's one thing. But to stop going out with me because of what other people do and say – that's something else entirely.

I like you. I mean, I *really* like you. I wouldn't have asked you out otherwise. You say you feel things deeply? Well, so do I. But I see your deep feelings don't extend in my direction. Please, Penny, don't do this. We're perfect for each other. I've never felt so comfortable with any other girl as I do with you. I can talk to you about anything. I don't have to put on a show or try and second guess you all the time. I don't want to lose that.

Can we meet up at our restaurant on Saturday? Say, eight o'clock? I think we should talk about this face to face.

Take care,

Robert

Dear Robert,

Can't we just be civilised about this and call it a day? I don't want to go out with you any more. I don't know how I can say it plainer than that. I don't understand why you can't see that this is for the best.

You say you feel comfortable with me? Well, I showed this letter to Gina and she agreed with me. The reason you feel comfortable with me is because you feel superior to me. I don't mean that in a nasty way. I'm not saying that you *deliberately* look down on me. But you don't see me as your equal. I know that in your own way you do like me – but why? Gina says it's because I'm not a threat. She says that you reckon no other boy could ever take me away from you. No other boy would ever want to.

Well, to be honest, I resent that. I'm not a charity case. I don't want you to go out with me because you feel sorry for me. So it's best if we just forget about going out together.

Please don't make this any harder than it has to be.

         Penny

Dear Penny,

I couldn't believe my eyes when I read your last letter. How dare you say that to me? I thought you knew me a lot better than that. It just shows how wrong one man can be. Your sister opens her mouth and spouts any old load of rubbish and you instantly believe her. Answer me this – how on earth can your poisonous sister know what's going on in my head? I asked you out because I liked you. I wanted to be with you because I liked you. That was all there was to it. Nothing more, nothing less.

We both know what you're doing now. You're just trying to find excuses for not going out with me. You're clutching at any straw your sister throws at you. And I'll tell you why. Because you *are* a coward. You were wrong about that one as well. So what if people look and stare and point? That's their look out, not ours. After the first couple of days of being with you, I didn't even notice – and that's the truth. You obviously did. You say you feel things deeply. I know that. What I didn't realise was that you allowed strangers to dictate how you should feel. I learnt a long time ago that you can't please everyone and if you try, you end up pleasing no one. So the only thing to do is please yourself. You're so busy trying to please your sister and your family, and Joe Bloggs who passes you on the street, that you and I have got lost somewhere in amongst all those people.

Penny, I still want to go out with you. I still care for you very, very much. I'm hoping that now you'll listen to me – and yourself. And no more letter writing please. Just phone me so we can talk about this, if not face to face then at least voice to voice.

All my love,

Robert

Malorie Blackman

Robert,

For goodness sake! Can't you take no for an answer? I don't want to go out with you any more. Is that so hard for your humungous ego to comprehend? We're just not right for each other. Why can't you accept that so that we can both move on? I showed Gina your letter and d'you know what she said? I told you so – that's what she said. She warned me from the time I started going out with you that we weren't right together and that the day would come when I would regret ever saying yes to you – and she wasn't wrong. She warned me how everyone would laugh at us – at me especially. I only wish I'd listened to her a lot earlier than I did.

I'm not going to write another letter. This is my last one. I see no point in dragging this out. It just makes it more painful for both of us. It's time to move on. If you can't – or won't – then that's up to you. As far as I'm concerned, you and I are an old book that I've closed. I have no intention of opening it again.

Penny.

Dear Penny,

Please don't think that this is a begging letter with me pleading for you to go back out with me. I realise that you've made up your mind and that's that. You've made a mistake – and that's not my ego talking.

Or rather that's not *just* my ego talking. You and I could have gone a lot further and been so much happier if you'd only given us a chance – but as you said, that's over now. An old book.

But let me say this. Maybe when you've finished cursing me and have had a chance to calm down and think about it, you'll begin to see the truth in what I'm saying.

Watch out for your sister. Gina's been poisoning your mind against the very thought of the two of us together from the very beginning. And I'll tell you why as well. She's a bigot. It wasn't some mythical man or woman in the street that was sneering at us – it was your sister. She's the one who couldn't bear to see us together. And she's the one who's succeeded in splitting us up. No, I take that back. She couldn't have done it if you hadn't let her.

I bet I can guess exactly what your sister thought the first time she saw us together.

'Oh my God! What's my sister doing with someone like *him*?'

And shall I tell you something else, Penny? Your sister is jealous of you. I can see your expression as you read that bit. I can just imagine the look of scorn and disbelief on your face, but it's true. Gina knows that if you gave yourself a chance you'd be much better than her in all the things that count. She's the one who keeps telling you that you can't do this, you shouldn't do that, you mustn't do whatever. She's the one holding you back by constantly being negative about everything you try to do and be. D'you remember when I tried to persuade you to come on holiday with my family? It was perfectly innocent and above board – my parents wouldn't allow anything else – and you almost said yes. But Gina talked you out of it.

'Penny, think of the two of you on holiday together. It just wouldn't work. You'd stick out like a hammered thumb. You'd spoil the holiday for everyone. You certainly wouldn't have a good time.'

Gina went on and on. I can still hear her, like a dripping tap. On and on and on. Until you gave in. Just as you always give in and do everything she says. She keeps telling you that you shouldn't draw attention to yourself. Well, why the hell not? Why should you try to blend in and be the same as everyone else? Is that really what you want for the rest of your life?

When the two of us went anywhere together, I was always so proud of you – your good looks, your beautiful smile. But you'd rather believe your sister's lies.

You'll have to forgive me if this letter sounds bitter, but I guess it is. I suppose it won't make much difference if I tell you this now but I will anyway. I want you to know something. I love you. All those times I kissed you and told you that I really liked you, inside I was saying I loved you. I'm sorry I never said it out loud. Maybe it would've made a difference. Maybe it wouldn't have made any difference at all. I guess we'll never know.

Anyway, take care of yourself and don't let Gina drag you down.

All my love,

Robert

Robert,

I know I said I wouldn't write to you again, but I just had to say this. If you think that you can get back with me by slagging off my sister, then you're deranged. I don't care if I never see you again.

Penny

Dear Robert,

How are you? I guess you're surprised to get a letter from me, especially after all this time and the last letter I wrote to you. I'm sorry about that. I've wanted to phone you and tell you how sorry I am about my last letter so many times, but I could never find the right words.

I was so happy to see you on Saturday. You looked very well. Even more great-looking than I remembered! I can't tell you how much I've missed you. The last eight months have crawled by. You were right of course. I was listening to everyone except myself. I still can't believe I could've got things so wrong.

Gina and I don't really talk much these days. A couple of months ago we were going for a meal when, across the street, Gina spotted a couple just like you and me.

'Look at that!' she said, shaking her head with disapproval.

Only then did she remember that she was with me instead of one of her other friends. I don't know which one of us was more shocked. She looked at me ruefully and we both laughed it off, but . . .

But.

I took out all your letters after that and read them and re-read them. It was as if I was just waking up. I can't believe I was so *stupid*. I look at Gina now and the way she felt about you and me is so obvious. I can read her every expression like one of those neon signs at Piccadilly Circus. Why couldn't I see it before?

Robert, I want to say I'm sorry. I'd like to say it face to face. Maybe we can meet up – any time, any place, anywhere. Just say the word.

Yours,

Penny

Dear Robert,

I'm not sure if you got my last letter. Although I didn't hear from you, I'm going to assume you did. I suppose I shouldn't really be surprised that you're still angry with me. I deserve it. But I know you're not one to hold a grudge.

That girl I saw you laughing with – is she your new girlfriend? I hope she isn't. There, I've said it. I'd really love to meet up with you again. What I mean is, I'd like to go out with you again.

I'm so sorry about the way I acted and the way I treated you. You deserved better than that. I'm sorry about a lot of things. I keep seeing Gina's face when we saw that couple like you and me. I still hear the words she said like Big Ben pealing in my head.

I know there are plenty of people out there who can't stand the thought of someone disabled going out with someone who isn't – but I never expected my sister to be one of them. You're one of the few people who noticed me first rather than my wheelchair. It's just a shame I didn't realise that eight months ago. Do write or phone or come and see me, Robert. I really would love to see you again. If that girl isn't your girlfriend then maybe we can pick up where we left off? Except I'd be different. I promise you, I won't use my wheelchair as an excuse or as a way of keeping you at arm's length.

Yours for ever,

Penny

Malorie Blackman

Dear Robert,

Don't worry, I'm not going to keep pestering you with letters. I wish I'd broken up with you face to face or over the phone. Writing it down was a big mistake on my part, wasn't it? If I'd told you I didn't want to go out with you any more, the words would've become hazy and blurred around the edges after all this time. Writing it all down has given you a permanently clear and sharp record of what I said. Do you re-read my letters at all? Do they still hurt as much? Maybe they just make you angry. Is that why you haven't contacted me? Maybe in your shoes I'd do the same thing.

I look at my wheelchair now and I hate it – more than I ever did before. It's a constant reminder of how I let it and my sister and a million silly things break us up. You'll never know how much I regret that.

Robert, I wish you the best of everything. Please, *please* do keep in touch. I'd love for us to be friends at least. Maybe you feel that's asking too much. I hope not. I know it's over between us as far as being an item is concerned, but I don't want to lose you completely.

Take care of yourself.

Ignore the smudges on the page.

       Love,

       Penny

Words Last For Ever

Dear Penny,

Can we meet up on Friday evening? We could go to our usual restaurant. We have a lot to talk about. A lot to sort out.

        All my love,

        Robert

Dear Robert,

Of course we can meet up. I can't wait.

        Yours for ever,

        Penny

Just Friends

Jamila Gavin

In the beginning, they were five. Five of them who started primary school together, moved up to the comprehensive together and turned into something of a gang. The word gang is probably too strong. It wasn't exclusive or menacing, they were just five friends growing up together and who, despite the changes, continued to like each other.

There was Emma, Clare, Ben, Nick and Tom. They were the core – although later, at the comprehensive, the circle often widened to include others. Each one at different times might hang out with other, newer friends. For a while, Emma saw no one but Jane; Clare found a mutual passion for riding with Rachel; and Ben and Nick both began having scenes with girls. Ben fancied Kate and went out with her for absolutely ages, whereas Nick enjoyed getting the reputation for playing the field. He was particularly good-looking – and when he was fourteen, he shot up so tall, that even older girls didn't mind going out with him.

Only Tom made no friends outside the group. He was a quiet lad; fond of music and serious about his work. So he confined himself to seeing which ever of his old friends was freewheeling at the time – and there was usually one of them.

In fact, it was Tom who became the kind of father figure of the group. He was a listener; happy to sit, always a little apart, watching his friends as they struggled with the ways of the world, giving his opinion when asked for it. It was Tom to whom they naturally turned with confidences. Emma wept on his shoulder when she was dropped by Richard – the first boy to ask her out and who she thought she loved. Clare asked his advice about how to deal with her mother's new boyfriend. Even Ben and Nick turned to Tom to chat things over about girlfriends, parents, teachers or sex.

The five of them looked out for each other. Nearly ten years of friendship – of sharing neighbourhood and school – meant that they were as concerned and devoted to each other's well being as if they were a family. For instance, they were alarmed when Clare began getting a bit wild. She had always been a trail-blazer, the one who had the ideas; the one who would say 'Hey you lot, why don't we . . .?' She was the first to smoke, the first to bring a bottle of vodka round one evening, and the first to try drugs.

The others were excited by the challenges she threw out to them. She set the pace and the others were only too glad to follow – except Tom. In the nicest possible way, Tom would just grin shyly and refuse the cigarette saying, 'You know me, I just can't stand the smell,' or, 'I don't think I want to rot my brains,' when he was offered alcohol, declaring that he preferred a cola. When one day a reefer of cannabis was passed round, it was the same. The shy shrug and the apologetic refusal – 'You know me! I'm just not into that sort of thing.'

Yet he was never judgemental. It was as though he didn't need to go through these rites of passage. 'You were born grown up, weren't you, Tom?' Clare teased him with a laugh.

One day Emma told the others that she had called round for Clare to find her drunk and hysterical. The group closed round protectively. Sitting in Tom's room in a blue haze of smoke and rave music playing on the tape deck, Clare managed to blurt out, 'Mum's boyfriend . . . well you know . . . he tried something.'

The group discussed her predicament long into the night. They all agreed that if Clare's mother wouldn't do anything and if the boyfriend continued to make advances, Clare would have to move out. 'You're sixteen now, you have the right,' said Tom. It was always Tom who knew the law.

'But where would I go?' wept Clare.

'You can come to me!' they chorused in unison.

It wasn't uncommon. There were people who would fall out with a parent and land up spending days or even weeks on the sofa of a friend.

Tom said, 'You can come here. Mum wouldn't mind – and we've tons of room.'

So Clare took to turning up for the odd few days when things got difficult at home.

'You've never really had a girlfriend have you, Tom?' Clare said one evening after she'd been telling Tom about her new boyfriend, Jake. 'Don't you fancy anyone?'

Tom smiled with slight embarrassment. 'I can't be bothered,' he said. 'I just don't want the hassle.'

'Yeah, I see what you mean,' laughed Clare, remembering all the boyfriends she had had. It wasn't all fun by any means. 'Jake's nice, though. Don't you think?' She probed him. It was important to all of them that Tom approved of their various relationships.

'Yeah, he seems OK,' Tom answered lightly, and that was good enough.

'His sister's really pretty – Melissa! I think she fancies you. When

Jamila Gavin

I told her that I sometimes stay round your place, she looked really interested. Do you hear, Tom?' Clare nudged him knowingly. 'Lots of boys fancy Melissa Parsons – but she'd go for you if you wanted.'

'I'll wait till the right girl comes along, thanks, Clare. She may be nice and she may be pretty – but, honestly – I'm not interested.'

They were all sixteen now and struggling with their GCSEs. They met up less as a group during the week – though they broke into twos or threes to help each other with homework. But they felt entitled to their weekends – come hell or high water – to seek out gigs or raves or parties.

However, despite parental misgivings, they all got comfortably through GCSE. Tom predictably got six As and three Bs, and everyone knew he was destined for university.

That summer, they all agreed to go Eurorailing together. They took weekend jobs and evening jobs, mostly waitressing or helping out at the supermarket to raise the money. When their exams were over, they pored over a map of Europe wondering if they could fit in both Amsterdam and Athens, the French Riviera and the Baltic coast.

They started in Amsterdam and that's when Emma and Tom found they shared a love of culture – or, to use their own terminology – found that they were both square.

'I've always wanted to see *The Night Watch*,' said Tom.

'The *what*?' cried Nick. 'Is that a group?'

'Dumb idiot,' jeered Emma. 'It's a painting by Rembrandt. I'd like to see it too. I'll go with you, Tom.' And that continued to be the pattern for the next six weeks as they made their way across Europe. Where the others wanted to head for the social scene, find the good clubs or, if they were anywhere near the sea, find the sun-soaked beaches, Emma and Tom found themselves splitting off from the others more and more, to look for the art galleries and museums and old churches.

That holiday set the two of them apart from the rest. It meant that they had different things to talk about. It meant that they built up their own confidences and their own vocabulary, and their names soon became linked – Tom 'n Em. But both quite cheerfully denied being an item. 'It would be like falling in love with my own brother,' giggled Emma when challenged by Clare.

Back home, Emma finally scotched any speculation, by falling madly in love with a passing traveller called Amos.

They were all fascinated by Amos. He seemed like a mixture between a gypsy and an Old Testament prophet. He was older than all of them – somewhere in his twenties. He had done his A-levels some time ago, it seemed – and even got a place at university; but he declared that all institutions were enemies of the people – and that the only pure life was one spent on the road, being beholden to no one. He claimed that he didn't even draw social security benefit, but mostly made money by busking or helping out on farms in the season. He was a magical musician, playing a guitar and singing heart-rending Irish folk songs. Dark-skinned, with henna-dyed dreadlocks, there was something deeply mysterious and compelling about him. He seemed a kind of Everyman, a man who had really lived and suffered. He'd been beaten up by police at the Battle of the Beanfields and seen the inside of a prison. It was said he came from a rich family and could have had everything he wanted, but was morally strong enough to give it all up. He believed in simplicity and no one ever saw him in anything other than his hand-knitted rainbow sweater, threadbare corduroys and well-worn boots. He had two lurcher dogs, called Castor and Pollux, who shadowed him off the lead wherever he went, and who obeyed his every command – they added to his image of someone with powers over man and beast.

The group discussed the travellers and their way of life intensively. They wondered whether they would find such a life appealing. Nick said, 'It might be all right for a bit – perhaps a year – but I'd start wanting my little luxuries after that, like a decent bath.'

Clare agreed. 'It's not being able to wash my hair when I want that would really get me down.'

'Always having to move on would bother me,' said Ben. 'They come at three in the morning – the police – and don't care if there are kids or whether it's raining. They come with their dogs and torches and batons, smashing up the place, looking for drugs. I couldn't stand all that.'

Emma was silent. That's when Tom knew that she was besotted with the man. He had thought it would pass – especially when it was known that the travellers' site had been raided by the police.

'Amos and his lot have been issued with a court order, haven't they, Em?' Tom asked gently.

Emma looked white and strained. 'Yeah! They've got to move on in ten days.'

'Where will they go?' exclaimed Nick.

'I think there's a friendly farmer over in Somerset. They can stay there for a bit,' she answered with bowed head.

'Huh!' cried Nick sceptically. 'The police know how to deal with "friendly" farmers all right. They won't last long there!'

'That's what I mean though,' cried Ben. 'I couldn't stand all the uncertainty of where I was going to be next.'

The group hardly saw Emma for the next ten days – except fleetingly, at school. Even then, she kept herself to herself and seemed to be deliberately avoiding them. But they knew – as everyone knew – that Emma was spending every possible moment down on the site with Amos.

Jamila Gavin

'Hey Em!' Tom called out to her one day as they were going home from school. 'Where've you been! I haven't seen you for ages!' Tom caught up with her, even though she seemed reluctant to wait for him.

'Ben, Nick and Clare are coming round tonight – and Clare's boyfriend, Jake. You will come too, won't you?'

Emma looked flustered. 'I . . . I don't think so, Tom. I promised to see Amos.'

'Bring him too,' persisted Tom.

But Emma refused to commit herself – and, at the railway bridge, they parted company; she to go on to the layby and Tom to go home through the town.

That evening, they all discussed Emma and expressed increasing anxiety about her infatuation with Amos. 'I've tried to warn her about him,' said Clare. 'I mean, he's too old for her and he's not one to be tied down. I've heard them talk about him. He's had loads of girls. But Emma's totally besotted. She doesn't care. She thinks this is different. She wants to live with him. She talks about their plans – how they're going to get hold of an old ambulance and convert it into their home. She says Amos is brilliant at making things.'

Ben snorted with disbelief. 'I find that hard to believe. You should see the state of his van.'

'All these years we've worried about Clare,' said Nick shaking his head. 'I just never dreamt that Emma would get involved with something like that. I mean she's so straight. Now, if she had fallen for Tom . . .' All heads turned to see Tom's reaction. Some of them had speculated among themselves whether Tom secretly fancied Emma.

Tom looked saddened and worried, but not distraught. 'She was going to have to break out of that cosy middle class family one of these days,' he commented philosophically. 'But she's intelligent. She'll come through.'

Emma's sudden departure though, shook them all to the core. No one dreamed that Em would go with him – not so soon. She hadn't even confided in Tom. They had thought she was the last person to opt out and bunk off her A-levels. It had always been Emma who had talked about going to art college, when others were still uncertain what they wanted to do.

Emma's parents were distraught. They came round and talked to the group pleading for information; desperate to learn where she might have gone. Apparently, they drove all over the country talking to groups of travellers. They looked everywhere for her without success. When she finally dropped them a card, it was to tell them she was all right, and they should not try to find her.

So there was nothing for her friends to do but to get on with working for their A-levels. When the exams were over, instead of hanging around waiting for the results, Tom took off. He took the ferry to Amsterdam.

Jamila Gavin

He went alone – and he went in an easy frame of mind. He allowed each day to dictate to him what he wanted. Somehow, he didn't want to make plans or be too systematic. If he felt like an art gallery, he went to an art gallery; if he felt like visiting a squat – he visited a squat. If he wanted to sit in a café by a canal for hours on end, he did. He had a month to wander about, and could have carried on into Germany and Switzerland, but something kept him in Amsterdam.

He remembered Emma and their summer together when they Eurorailed two years ago. What had happened to her? He remembered their companionship; the alleys they had walked; the bridges they had looked over. He remembered all those art galleries and historic buildings and churches, which only she in the group had wanted to explore with him. Funny how you can know someone all your life – think you know them – and then suddenly, a blank; they've gone like a puff of smoke, as if all those years had counted for nothing.

It was on his third visit to *The Night Watch* that he saw her.

At first he didn't recognise her. He saw her from behind, looking like a regular traveller – her hair dyed henna and very frizzed out; a long Indian skirt and tasselled jacket; long woollen tights and boots. But it wasn't the clothes which disguised her, it was her thin, thin body. He could see her shoulder blades from behind, sticking out like wings. He walked up warily, still not recognising her, but nevertheless drawn to her. She had sat down cross-legged in front of the huge canvas, oblivious to the visitors swirling around, and the troupes of tourists being lectured to by their guides.

He came level with her and stood close by, then looked her full in the face. 'Em?'

He had hurried her out of the gallery for, at the sight of him, tears had poured down her face. They walked and talked all day. At nightfall, she took him back to her squat – yes, she lived in a squat along with several others. She managed to earn a bit of money working in a tulip bulb factory. Amos wasn't there. No, he had gone months ago. He hadn't even told her. She couldn't face going home in this state, feeling so humiliated. She wanted to try and get back on her feet first.

Tom stayed the night in the squat. It was just an abandoned shell of a building choking with rubble and dust. It had no running water or electricity and broken windows rattled in their rotting frames. The smell and the damp and the cold made Tom want to flee, but he didn't have the heart and, after whispered conversations long into the night, they slept fitfully, back to back in sleeping-bags, snuggled together under a duvet.

The brazier of burning charcoal cast long desperate shadows of others who crouched over glowing embers, passing reefers to each other and snorting their substances.

Next morning Tom pleaded with Emma: 'You must come back with me. You'll be OK. It's awful here. Home must be better than this. You could still do your A-levels and go to art college, just as you always planned.'

'Amsterdam is like a huge art college!' laughed Emma. 'The world is my art college. Do you think Van Gogh did A-levels and went to art college? Course not! He just worked and lived and painted and . . .'

' . . . And was poverty stricken and went mad and chopped off his ear and died in an asylum.' Tom finished off for her bitterly.

Later, after they had had a final walk round the city and were leaning over their favourite bridge, Em said shyly, 'Isn't it stupid that you and me aren't – you know – in love with each other? I mean, we're so suited. We like the same things; we never quarrel. You're my best friend, Tom . . .' Her eyes filled with tears.

Tom sighed and squeezed her arm. 'Yeah. I've thought the same sometimes. Love doesn't seem to be about getting along, does it?' He remembered Amos. 'It's about something quite different. Something you know about, Em, and I don't.'

'Do you think you'll ever marry, Tom?' Emma asked.

'Probably, but I don't want to think about it yet. I want to go to university first, and I want to travel.' He gazed down into the shifting waters of the canal. They both let the silence drift. Then Tom said, 'I tell you what. If you and I are still free in five years time, let's meet here. On this bridge in Amsterdam, and let's see then whether . . .'

'Whether?' Em whispered.

'Well, whether you and me should be an item.'

They hugged each other, not with passion, but with all the years of love and friendship that they shared. Then they parted; she walked off the bridge one way, he the other. Before they lost sight of each other, they both instinctively turned. 'See you in five years – here, this date, this time!' Then they were gone.

Letter from Kalymnos

Michael Morpurgo

24 August 1995

Dear Zo,

I've been trying to write to you for some time, but until now I haven't known what to say or how to say it. But I must write it now.

I expect you hate me after what I've done. I certainly couldn't blame you if you did. I just hope that, when you've read this letter, you'll understand why I did what I did, and then maybe you won't hate me quite so much.

All my life, the part of it I can remember, you've been my best friend, ever since St John The Baptist Junior School, class one – Miss Parmenter's class. Who could forget Miss Parmenter, with her spectacles cut in half so that she could look daggers at you over the top? She caught me writing 'bum' on the back of my hand, and then she caught you giggling at it. I was always getting you into trouble. We both had to write 'bum' a hundred times and take it to the head teacher so we wouldn't think it was funny any more. It didn't work, did it? Every class we were in, we always managed to sit next to each other, and you let me copy you whenever I needed to, which was often. Once we got to Pretoria Street Comp we still stuck together. We engineered it so that we both did French and English and Archaeology right through to the sixth form. Silly really, because I was always hopeless at French. I still am.

And it wasn't just at school we stuck together. Home was wherever we ended up at four o'clock, your place or mine. When you had your glandular fever that time and you were in bed for a month, I came and read to you every day – Babar. I know those stories by heart. Whenever I think of elephants now, I think of you and glandular fever. Then, when Mum went into one of her depressions, you'd always be over at my place, and we'd clean up the house together to make her feel better; and when we'd finished, we'd lie on my bedroom floor and just talk. You'd tell me your secrets, and I'd tell you mine, most of them anyway. We were always together. And when my dad went off, I called you and you came round and I cried up against you. You told me we can't pick our parents, only our friends. I'd never thought of that. You told me

Michael Morpurgo

that you'd never desert me, no matter what; and you kept your word. It was me that deserted you. But I didn't just desert you, did I? I betrayed you. I cheated you.

Boys. It was the only thing we really didn't see eye to eye about. I always thought you were so strange about them. You never looked at them. They just didn't seem to interest you, until Daniel. Not like me at all. I was never happy unless I had two or three of them chasing me. I knew you never liked the head hunter in me, but you never said anything. I don't remember you judging me, not once in all the time I've known you. I just thought the whole boy thing was a big game, and there weren't any rules. You made them up as you went along. You knew it wasn't like that, and you were right. I just didn't know it then, that's all.

More than anything, I want you to believe that what I did wasn't intentional. It just happened. Even that first day when you brought him into school – Daniel Duroy, your French exchange – you were like the cat that got the cream. You adored him. I could see that. Everyone could. I couldn't see why. I mean, he was all right to look at, nothing special. He was no Gérard Depardieu, was he? He was silent and unsmiling too. He scarcely seemed to notice I was there, and I wasn't used to that. You were happier for those three weeks than I'd ever seen you. You glowed, and I was so jealous. I think you knew I was too. It was because I missed you. You were always with him, wrapped

Letter from Kalymnos

up in him. You hardly noticed me all the time he was there. And once he'd gone home, you talked about nothing except Daniel and how wonderful he was, how kind, how sensitive, how intellectual, how unlike any other boy you'd ever met. We had first-year-sixth exams coming up and you didn't even swot. I'd never known you like it.

Then you got ill again with your glandular fever and you cried because the doctor wouldn't let you go back for your three weeks in France with Daniel. And what did you do? You asked if I would like to go in your place. Daniel liked me – he'd told you so. You'd go over and see him at Christmas instead maybe. That's how much you trusted me.

I didn't really want to go. I don't much like speaking French, and I wasn't sure how I would get on with Daniel. But it was three weeks away from school. And you'd told me his place was by the sea, you'd shown me the photos. Besides, anything would be better than hanging around home with Mum. She doesn't seem to mind whether I'm home or not, just so long as she has enough drink in the house. I had some money saved up. So I went.

The schools in France had already finished for the summer holidays. I don't think Daniel knew what to do with me at first. We hardly spoke, because I wouldn't try out my French; and, anyway, he seemed happy enough with silence. So I didn't make the effort.

He showed me round Concarneau. We saw the castle together.

Michael Morpurgo

That was the last time I wrote to you, the day we went round the castle. We sent you a postcard of it, and we signed it together. I remember it because that was the moment I first knew I loved him. We were sitting on the quay in the sun, watching the yachts going in and out, dangling our legs over the side. I handed him your card to sign. There was a seagull eyeing us sideways. We laughed, and then we looked at each other and we loved each other. I can't explain it. I still can't.

After that I spoke English and he spoke French – we found it easier that way. We just talked and walked and talked and walked. His mother and father were never home, so when we weren't at the beach snorkelling and swimming, we were at home sitting on the lawn drinking cold apricot juice and talking. Not just talking; touching, kissing, loving. Not the groping and grappling I'd done before. He didn't know what he was doing any more than I did, but we managed. We managed together. Best of all was sleeping curled up into his back and waking to find him still there. I'd blow gently on the hair at the back of his neck until he woke. And we laughed, how we laughed. Not at anyone, not at each other; but because we were so happy, so completely right for each other.

Whenever his mother and father came home from work – I still don't know what they did, he had something to do with boats I think – we were always on our best behaviour again. We'd hold hands under

Letter from Kalymnos

the table and squeeze secret signals at one another. They're a bit prim and proper, and always busy-busy – the kitchen, the garden, the car. He was always washing the car. They have one of those cars that rises up on its wheels when it starts. It always made me giggle.

I'm telling you all this, Zo, not to make you angry, although I know it must, but because I want you to know how it was between us, how it was natural, right and good. After the first few heady days we began to talk a lot about you, and I told him often how we had nothing to feel guilty about. But no matter how hard I tried to reason it out and justify it so that I shouldn't feel guilty, I did, and so did Daniel.

I expect you began to wonder what was going on when you didn't hear any more after the card from Concarneau, but I just couldn't face telling you what had happened. When I didn't come back at the end of the three weeks, I knew you must have guessed. And by then I couldn't bring myself to tell you because I knew you knew, and I knew how much you'd be hating me.

I was due to catch the boat back home on the Sunday from Roscoff, but I just couldn't bear to leave him. I pretended to be ill, unfit to travel, stomach upset. Daniel's mother and father believed it. Why shouldn't they? As they said, English people often get stomach upsets in France. I phoned Mum and told her I'd be back as soon as I was better. She didn't seem bothered one way or the other. She never even asked me what it was I'd eaten or anything. From her voice I think she was drinking again. I really hate her when she's like that. I know it's not her fault, but I can't help myself. One thing's for sure. At least I'll never grow up like her.

During my 'illness', Daniel worked out a plan. It was simple. We'd go off together backpacking for as long as we could. We would go as far as his money would stretch. He'd done it before, so his parents wouldn't be worried about it. I told them Mum had said it was all right for me to stay on a while after I got better. They went along with it without a murmur. Too busy washing cars and cleaning kitchens to worry about it, I think. So we set off.

Three days and four nights later, we found ourselves here in Kalymnos, a little Greek island off the coast of Turkey. I sent a card to Mum, told her that I was better and that I'd be back before term began again. I knew she'd be mad at me for doing it, but I didn't care. I left no address, so we were on our own and no one knew where we were. We'd bought as much time as we needed. I did a bit of waitressing in the evenings in a café on the seashore. It paid the rent on the room we shared with a million mosquitoes. We swam and we made love, and we swam and we made love. I don't know why they call it seventh heaven, but if there is one, then we were there, for more than a month we were there, and it was wonderful.

It was Daniel's birthday and I knew he loved to go diving. There was a wonderful blue and white caique moored in the harbour, a diving-boat. It didn't cost much to go out for the day. It was my birthday present to him.

We went out on the most beautiful day I ever saw. The sea was a flat, calm, jade green over the sand, blue further out. There wasn't a whisper of wind, not a puff of cloud. We chugged out and dropped anchor in a bay along the coast. There were just a few flat-topped houses and a café beyond the beach. I lazed on the deck sunbathing while Daniel got himself all togged up. He flip-flopped around the deck, snorting into his breathing apparatus. Then he flapped his flipper at me and went over the side, a ten-metre dive, the instructor told me.

There was another couple on board the caique, Italians. He was called Enrico and she was called Gina. They were both beautiful. Everything was beautiful that day. Daniel came up after half an hour or so, climbed on board and dripped all over me as he pulled his gear off. He looked like a god against the sun, my god. Olive skin, grey eyes, gorgeous. Laughing down at me, he told me I should try it, that it was so peaceful at the bottom of the sea, that you were really alone down there. I said I didn't want to be alone, that I wanted to be with him for ever. The instructor patted him on the shoulder to congratulate him, and then busied himself with the Italians as they prepared for their dive. That was when Daniel said he was thirsty and asked me if I wanted a drink. 'Coke,' I told him. The next thing I heard was a great splash, and when I stood up I saw he was swimming for the beach a hundred or so metres away. I remember wondering how he was going to manage to swim back all that way with a can of Coke in his hand. I watched him powering through the sea. He swam so well. He was made for it.

I dozed off while he was gone, not proper sleep, just thinking. I was thinking of you, Zo. I was always thinking of you and wondering how I was ever going to face you again. Then a shadow came over me. It was the instructor asking after Daniel. I told him where he had gone, and he frowned, shook his head and turned away from me. 'He shouldn't have,' he said. 'I told him. Every time you go down deep, stay out of the water for at least an hour after. I *told* him.'

He scanned the beach and the café with his binoculars. He called in the Italians and started up the engine. We were going looking for Daniel. I didn't see why he should be so worried. I wasn't. I knew Daniel swam like a fish.

The fishermen mending their nets had not seen him on the beach. He hadn't been seen in the café. We could see no one swimming out in the bay. One of the fishermen shook his head and told us where we should look. He would come and help. They would all come and help. He knew. They all knew, except me. I was still wondering what all the fuss was about. Daniel had clambered ashore somewhere and was making his way to the café. We just couldn't see him from where we were, that's all. But no one was searching the island, no one was looking on the shore. I watched from the deck of the caique. I kept telling the instructor they were all looking in the wrong place, that Daniel was ashore already. He said nothing. He didn't seem to want to look at me. They were all out in boats now, scouring the bay, leaning over and peering down into the sea.

The Italians were snorkelling in the shallows around one of the fishing boats when they found him.

I was there when they dragged him out and tried to revive him, but they never tried hard enough. They just gave up. I tried mouth to mouth, but they pulled me off him. Gina sat by me on the deck as we went back to port, her arm round me, and I looked at the dirty green tarpaulin that covered him, still hoping that it was all a nightmare, that any moment now the tarpaulin would move and Daniel would throw it off and sit up. I could see one of his feet. I willed his toes to move, but they never did.

Back at the harbour, the police were waiting with an open van. There were boxes of tomatoes in the back. They put him on a stretcher and laid him out in the van in the sun alongside the tomatoes. There were dozens of people crowding round, all wanting a look. I said I had to go with him in the van, but they wouldn't listen. They wouldn't let me go with him. They took him away from me, and I never saw him again.

There were questions, lots of questions, about how it had

happened, where he came from, where I came from. They took his passport and everything that was his, and left me alone in our room. That was when I really understood that he was dead for ever, gone from me, that I was quite alone in the world.

For two days now I've been here. I haven't moved from our room. Gina and Enrico are kind. They bring me food, grapes, and grilled fish and bread. But I don't want to eat and I can't seem to make them understand that. They sit with me, but we can't speak to one another. So they hug me long and hard, and cry, and then they leave me. And I'm alone again.

Daniel's mother and father will be here tomorrow, that's what the police told me. I suppose they'll take the body back to France. I don't want to see them. They'll blame me, and they'd be right to blame me. If I hadn't come instead of you, if I hadn't taken him away from you, if we hadn't been lovers, then Daniel would still be alive.

The light has gone out of my life, and I am alone in utter darkness. Daniel is gone. So I will go too. I will go down to the bay he drowned in. I will breathe in the sea water that he breathed in, and I'll go to be with Daniel wherever he is. If it's heaven, then we'll be there together. If it's not, if it's nowhere, if it's darkness, then I'd rather be in darkness with Daniel than alone and without him for the rest of my life.

Do you know that you're the only person in the world I'll miss? I think you're the only one who really knows me or cares. And look what

Letter from Kalymnos

I did to you. That's why I've written to you. Because I want you to forgive me. It's all I care about now.

I think it'll be easy. I hope so. I'll just walk into the sea and keep walking. I'm not frightened, Zo, really I'm not. You will forgive me, please?

Love,

Selina

The House that Darren Built

Carlo Gébler

Darren's first memory was when he was two years old. He was in the Army quarters where they lived then, near Aldershot, mother, father, himself. He was in the living-room. The fire was out. He was cold.

He tottered into the hall and climbed the stairs on all fours. On the landing he found his mother's bedroom door and pushed it open.

She was lying on the bed. She was snoring. There was a terrible smell. He didn't know it then but later he would be able to identify this as alcohol and vomit.

He shouted at the figure, shouted and shouted. Nothing woke her. She was dead to him. One of the army wives passing outside heard him. Some bossy women came and took him away. He didn't remember

The House that Darren Built

much of this, or much at all of the next stretch of his life. Well, he did remember his father coming and talking to him. Something about a new wife, a new family. Nothing spelt out but Darren knew the score. There was going to be no room for him in the new nest. This quite often happened to him – he saw things before they happened. Then it was like he went to sleep – and he didn't wake up until he was ten years old.

He was living with John and Angela then, his foster-parents. Nice people, very religious. They had three rules – no drinking, no smoking, no driving.

Every summer they would take the train to Taunton for a cycling holiday in the West Country. Whenever they cycled by a line of cars backed up in a traffic jam, as they did frequently, John would shout, 'See, Darren, never drive a car. You just waste time, like these mugs.'

Darren couldn't agree. He liked the look of the shiny cars – even if they weren't going anywhere. So, once the hols were over and he was back home, Darren made friends with the son of their minister – he was into rallying. Darren learnt how to take a car to pieces, put it back together again, and when he was older, he learnt how to drive one. Made one or two dodgy garage contacts as well. John and Angela were hurt, of course, by Darren's car mania, but understanding too. They were like that; knew how to live and let live. And their home was his, wasn't it? And he was family. He had to be given his space. That's what you did with family. That's what they always said. And meant.

But then real family moved in. This was Angela's mother. She was senile, incontinent, sometimes violent, given to wandering off in the middle of the night wearing nothing but her nightdress. The house was tiny. John and Angela didn't want what happened next but they didn't believe they had any alternative. With mother taking all their time, they had no space for Darren. They asked him to go. He went to a home. He was sixteen.

In Appleton Lodge there were twenty young people. But Darren only had eyes for Sophy. Tall, blonde, beautiful. He thought she was brilliant. They started to smoke together – tobacco and marijuana; and drink together, cider, then vodka; they started to fool around together. Sophy let him touch her breasts some nights. He thought she was brilliant.

One day, he got a foolish notion to buy her a ring. He was on a YTS scheme, getting work experience in a car showroom. He swept the floor, mopped the toilet. Apparently, this would teach him all about retailing.

He took a few quid from the till, bought Sophy a Claddagh ring. A cheapo. She wasn't impressed. So he fancied getting her something else. Bigger. Something really expensive.

The House that Darren Built

One night, walking back to Appleton Lodge, he saw a woman pull up outside a Spar shop and run inside with her kid.

Key in the ignition, engine still running. Like taking candy from a baby. He got in and drove away and went straight round to see one of his dodgy garage contacts. The car he'd stolen was a Renault station wagon. He got seven hundred quid. Darren couldn't believe his luck.

Back at Appleton Lodge, he flashed his wad at Sophy and the others. Big mistake. Word got back to the warden. His room was searched, the money was found. Plus, the police were making inquiries. He'd been seen getting into the car he stole. Everything fell into place and he was arrested. A week before his sixteenth birthday, Darren was up before the beak.

He got ten months inside. Hell. First day in the YOI he got his head stuffed down the toilet. Then he fell out with the main man. He had a packet of Rothmans and he wouldn't hand them over. So he got whacked, twice. The main man used a sock full of billiard balls. Broke Darren's nose. Taught him a lesson though. You didn't walk alone. You couldn't survive. He made friends with the car thieves. Learnt everything they could tell him. Plus enjoyed their protection. When he left he had a trade. He was a graduate of the university of crime.

Social Services put him in a bed-sit. He was lonely. All he had was his benefit. He went for three jobs, apprentice mechanic. Same story every time. 'Look, son, we'd love to help you but you understand, not with your record we can't . . .'

He started stealing cars; first on the principle that he needed to eat; later in order to drink. One night he got absolutely plastered on a half-one of vodka, two Thunderbirds, and a pint of cider. Wandering the streets, out of his mind, he saw a tasty Mercedes, series six.

He got in quick and drove off. This wasn't stealing; he was just going to take her for a spin. Just round the block and then take her back and leave her where he found her. But she was such a lovely drive. Handled beautifully.

Next thing he was on the motorway. Heading he didn't know where. He was vaguely aware of cars speeding past him, lights flashing, horns blaring. Later he was aware of police cars on the hard shoulder, and policemen waving frantically at him. He put his foot down. Then he heard four bangs. Didn't know what they were. Then he felt the rumbling noise, the unmistakable sound of a flat. Actually he had four of them. The Merc wasn't going anywhere now. He had to stop. The police marksmen who'd shot the tyres out were around him in seconds.

They hauled him out, cuffed him. He'd been driving down the motorway on the wrong side. Driving under the influence. Driving without due care and attention. Driving recklessly with intent to endanger life. There were twenty-three charges on the sheet.

'I don't know what we're going to do with you,' said the probation

The House that Darren Built

officer assigned to his case. 'They're going to kill you in court. You're going down for two or even three years. You'll be twenty-one when you get out and all you'll have to show for the last five years is a working knowledge of prison.'

He went to a bail hostel. Eight o'clock curfew. Nothing to do in the evening, just hang around the hall. Drink was forbidden of course, but sometimes he'd cadge a bottle off one of the others. Drink was great because drink really got you out of it.

One evening, feeling particularly low, he was hanging about the hall hoping to make a connection.

There was no one around, no one to talk to. He began to read the notices on the notice-board. Usual sort of stuff about AIDS, learning to read, what to do if you're pregnant. Then it caught his eye. Top left-hand corner. A scheme for prisoners to build themselves a house and afterwards rent the house. The Prisoners' Housing Trust. Like in a cartoon strip, the light bulb went on over his head. It was like suddenly he saw ahead.

The probation officer thought it was a great idea and he sent Darren for an initial interview. This involved sitting in a room with a load of suits from the Trust and answering questions. Darren managed that hurdle easy.

Next he was sent with some other young crims to a camp. Something to do with the Duke of Edinburgh Awards. He and a few others had to build a raft with a few planks and a couple of drums. A pushover. Knew what to do at once. Got everyone pulling together. Had it done in an hour. He was in.

Back in court, the magistrates issued a probation order.

'You did well,' the probation officer said afterwards, shaking Darren's hand.

Darren's new foster-family went by the name of Huggins; Jeffrey and Deidre were the father and mother; three children, two away and one still at home, Karen. The first time he met her Darren thought she wasn't bad. Fair hair, a bit plump. Didn't exactly turn him on though. And besides, he had something else on his mind.

The following day was Monday. The probation officer collected him, brought him to the site for eight o'clock. It was on a piece of wasteland at the end of a suburban street. The supervisor was an old bloke, John to everyone else but Mr Prentice to him. There were two other crims there as well, older fellows who were going to work with them.

The site had been prepared. A lorry came and dumped its load of ready mix. The four of them raked the concrete into place. The blocks arrived and he had a day with an instructor – before starting each stage someone would come and teach him what to do. Darren learnt how to mix concrete and use a plumb and set a level, and then he and the other two men and Mr Prentice began to build, block on block. Walls slowly rose with spaces for doors and windows. He was actually

The House that Darren Built

building himself a house. It was absolutely wicked. He felt better than he'd ever felt in his life before.

Two weeks in, they had their first visit from building control. Darren was up on a scaffolding board when the car drew up, the bloke got out with his clipboard, and came on to the site.

Mr Prentice knew him.

'Hello, John,' said the stranger.

'Hello, Stanley,' said Mr Prentice.

'I don't know why I do this job,' said the man from building control. 'My job is to stop houses falling down. To make certain that if there's a fire, you can get out. But does anyone ever thank you? No, never, I'm just a problem. I'm just the guy who makes you spend money putting in a fire door or moving a window. I'm like a lightning conductor for everyone's hatred. And just recently, you know, you know my wife, you know Chloe . . .'

'Course I do,' said Mr Prentice sympathetically.

'She's started saying she doesn't think she can go on living with a lightning conductor any more. I don't know what I'm going to do.'

Standing on the scaffolding boards, just above the men, Darren worked away as quietly as he could, and as he worked he listened. He drank in every word. He'd heard talk like this before, just never paid much attention. Perhaps that's what happened when you got older? You could hear what you couldn't hear before.

'Get down here,' shouted Mr Prentice, and he scooted down.

'This is Stanley – Mr Hall to you, building control.'

The man put his hand out. He was mid-fifties, face like a crumpled bag, kind of sad looking.

Darren shook the man's hand. At the same time he got that feeling again when he had a sense of the future, like he had when his father last came to see him, like he got in the bail hostel when he read the notice on the notice-board. This grumbling old bloke, Mr Hall – he was going to feature in his life in some important way.

When Darren went home that evening he knocked on Karen's bedroom door, went in, sat down on her bed and told her. You could do that with Karen. Tell her things. She listened well. Talked nicely too.

There was also something different about her. Everyone else was into rave and techno, but she was into Grease and Saturday Night Fever. Huge picture of John Travolta over her bed, black leather jacket, killer blue eyes. She had the cassettes, played him the songs. Darren sang along.

Karen looked at him sort of curiously and he half-wondered if she thought he was coming on to her. Nah. She lived in the house where he had a room. She was a good laugh and good for a chat. Nah, he wasn't interested in Karen. Nah. How could he be interested in a girl who liked John Travolta?

The next bit at the house was even more brilliant than the blocks.

That was just the skeleton; now what he did was put flesh on that skeleton, adding the doors and walls and windows and ceilings and a roof – all the things that made a house a house.

He felt happy. Same time, he couldn't help noticing, he was getting something for Karen. Sort of liking her. Nothing serious. No, definitely, nothing serious. He was just getting to like her. More.

Looking forward to seeing her all the time, and all. Actually, when the evening came, he couldn't wait to go home to her. And when he got home to the Huggins', he always went straight to Karen's room, knocked on her door, went in and sat down on the bed under the poster of John Travolta, and told her about his day. But it wasn't just a one way street. Him blabbing, her listening. Sometimes they spent hours playing her quiz game, musical chairs. You had to answer questions about musicals while you moved counters round the board. Karen always won but Darren didn't mind.

Back at the house, the walls, windows, doors and roof, were all done, and now it was time for the plumbing and the electrics. Mr Hall was usually there every day, moaning to John Prentice about his life and his marriage, but he always made a point, did Mr Hall, of talking to Darren, about his work, the family he lodged with, Karen. They were palsy, quite palsy really, which was different really, when you considered, one was a miserable old bloke, and the other was young.

But one particular day they stopped for sandwiches at twelve, like they always did, and Mr Prentice and Mr Hall sat together. Mr Prentice gave his friend from building control a hard-boiled egg. Mr Prentice shelled his egg but he didn't eat it. He was talking too much.

'I keep coming home to find my wife sitting in the kitchen,' said Mr Hall. 'She'll sit in the kitchen and she'll stare out at the garden. It gets dark – but Chloe won't even bother to get up and turn on the light.

'My two girls know something's wrong,' he continued. 'They keep looking at me, desperately. We don't talk. We don't have any money. I paid more for my house than I could sell it for now. But I gotta pay the mortgage. I'm just keeping afloat but I don't know if I've got the energy to keep going.'

'Course you have,' said Mr Prentice soothingly.

And Darren wanted to shout out, 'Course you've got the strength to keep going.' Only he didn't. Well he couldn't, could he? They'd mark him for a snoop then and they'd be on their guard after that.

Of course, when he got home he told Karen. Everything. And she understood about wanting to shout out but being frightened of the consequences. Over the weeks and months he and Karen definitely grew closer.

Then he had an idea. 'Let's go camping,' he said.

He went and asked the parents, 'May Karen and I go camping on the Isle of Wight?'

He had ferry times and bus times; he had the name of a campsite;

most important of all, he had a sleeping plan. Two separate tents. Karen's parents thought that made the trip OK. And it *was* their intention to sleep separately.

Unfortunately, there was a storm and Karen's tent was rubbish. It let rain in at the seams. By the bucket load. In an hour, Karen's sleeping-bag was soaked.

She ran over to Darren's tent, crawled in, woke him up. Her nightdress was soaking. He gave her a dry T-shirt to change into and, as she pulled off her wet nightdress, he saw her breasts and her long white thighs by torchlight. And she saw he saw.

He unzipped his sleeping-bag. Opened it out. They were just going to lie underneath it. They were just going to lie underneath it and go to sleep. That's what they agreed. Only the smell of Karen's hair. The warmth of her skin. The sound of her heart and her breathing. It did something to him. He couldn't help himself. Actually, it did something to the both of them. They were in this together and they couldn't help themselves. Course they knew they shouldn't, and, what's more, they knew that if they did they should take precautions. But they'd never felt anything like this before. It pushed all reason out of their thoughts. It was like a wave had crashed on to the shore, plucked them up, and thrown them far out to sea. It was overwhelming, and when they woke up the next morning, there they were together, naked, under the sleeping-bag.

On Sunday night, they went back to Karen's. Walking on air. Cloud nine. Arrived on time, exactly as they said they would. Said nothing to Karen's parents of course. Natch. Just the trip was good, the weather was awful.

But inside they were glowing. The glow lasted three weeks. Then Karen's period didn't come and didn't come and didn't come. She got a predictor kit, did the test. Pink. She was pregnant.

'I'm pregnant,' she told Darren, when he got back from the site.

Darren felt like he did after the arrest on the motorway when he was cuffed. He thought he was going to be sick. He wanted the ground to open up and swallow him. Long forgotten prayers from the John and Angela times came back to him.

They went downstairs together. They blurted out the truth. Karen's mother said nothing.

'I shall discuss this with your probation officer,' said Mr Huggins, when he came home later. He was icy, terrifyingly icy. 'Now get out of my sight. Go to your room and stay there, because I don't want to set eyes on you for the rest of the evening.'

Darren went to his room, lay on his bed. He heard Karen crying downstairs. He heard Deidre saying, 'Why?' over and over again, 'Why? Why?' He wanted to pack his bag, bunk out the window, do a runner.

But then a still small voice inside his head spoke up – one he'd never heard before.

The House that Darren Built

'What do you want to do that for, Darren?' said the voice (which did sound a bit like Mr Prentice and John and Angela and his probation officer all rolled up in one). 'You do a runner and you'll be breaking the conditions of the court. You'll lose the house, and you'll go to prison. You mightn't ever see Karen again.'

Next morning, when he woke up, Darren knew just what to do. Exactly. The business about sleeping on a problem was right.

He was on site and waiting for Mr Prentice when the older man arrived at eight o'clock. 'Listen,' said Darren, and he told him the story. Well, some of it. He said he had a girlfriend, she was pregnant, she was expecting a baby, and they were going to live together. Therefore, he had to change the house plans. Adapt to circumstances. He had to put in a cupboard in the hall for a pram. He needed low hooks for a child to hang his coat. (The baby would be a boy, he knew that.) He needed to add two gates, one at the bottom of the stairs, one at the top. He had ideas. Could he make some sketches? Actually physically alter the plans?

Mr Prentice said all right. Mr Hall showed up and added his tuppence worth while Darren was at work. The gates couldn't close with a latch, he said. Had to shut with a magnet. That way, in a fire, they could just push open.

'Thank you, Mr Hall,' said Darren.

'I like you, Darren,' said Mr Hall.

In the evening, Darren brought the plans home, showed them to Mrs Huggins.

'I love your daughter,' he explained. 'I want us to live together. The three of us. I'm serious.'

Deidre said nothing. But when her husband pitched in later, he heard Deidre saying to him, behind the closed kitchen door this was, 'I think he's serious about Karen, and from what she's said to me, she's serious about him.'

'I don't want to know,' said Mr Huggins. 'I shall be saying to his probation officer, get him out of here. He's betrayed our trust.'

'I know,' agreed Deidre, 'but he's trying to make amends. Look at the plans he's made,' continued Deidre. 'Doesn't that show something? Just look at them. Just look.'

'I want him out.'

'No, don't throw him out. Not without giving him a hearing. Just wait. Only a week. Anyway, you can't just throw him out. One, he's nowhere to go, and two, you have to think about Karen.'

The next few months at the Huggins' house were arctic. The thaw was very, very slow to come but it came, in the end, it came.

On the site, meanwhile, the work went on, over the autumn, over the winter (they were inside the house by now, it was planned that way) and into the next spring. The baby came in March. It was a boy. They called him Mervyn. He had squashy ears and dark eyes. The

The House that Darren Built

house was nearly finished. Walls plastered and painted, kitchen fitted, everything in working order. There was even a frieze up on the wall in the room they'd earmarked for the baby. Only one remaining hurdle. House had to be signed off by building control. Then it was finished. Darren and Karen could move in.

Mr Hall came out to do the business. It was a Friday, early in the summer. Mr Prentice and the others had gone home. Darren was there on his own, fiddling with the aerial up on the roof. He came down and they shook hands. Mr Hall was agitated and unhappy as usual. Nothing said but Darren knew. It was the house and money and the mortgage, and his wife threatening to leave him, and his two daughters – fourteen year old girls – who saw the divorce looming and wanted him to do something. Mr Hall saw it too but he didn't know what to do. He felt dreadful. Also, some hooligan had thrown an ice-cream at his window on the way out to the site, and now the ice-cream had dried in the sun on the windscreen.

'I'll wash it off for you,' said Darren.

'You're very kind,' said Mr Hall. 'Thank you.'

'Can I talk to you?' Mr Hall asked.

'Course.'

'Can I ask you how you came here? What did you do? What happened when you were a child? It's nosy, I know, and I shouldn't ask, but I've heard little bits and pieces.'

77

'Are you going to sign the house off?'

'Course.'

So they went inside and he made them both a mug of tea, and he told Mr Hall the story, from the very start.

And the funny thing was, as he told Mr Hall the story, Darren could tell the older man was eating out of his palm, listening to every word he, Darren, said, and the old bloke had nothing else whatsoever on his mind.

It occurred to Darren that, while he was talking, all Mr Hall's worries were banished, and he was on holiday from himself. And maybe that's what falling in love had done to Darren. Love had made him see things about other people which he'd never noticed before.

And when the story was over Mr Hall said, 'That was very really interesting. Thank you for the tea. Your place is signed off.' He shook Darren's hand and went out whistling.

He got into his car and as he drove home, Mr Hall thought the same thing Darren had thought; while he'd been listening, he'd been on holiday from himself, and when he realised that, a feeling rose up in him that he hadn't known for years. Hope. If he could escape his unhappiness for an hour, then it was possible to escape it for ever.

As soon as he got home he went and found his wife. She was sitting in the kitchen on one of the kitchen stools and staring sadly out at the garden. He put his arms round her, and he told her that

The House that Darren Built

he'd been away but that now something had happened, he'd rounded the corner, and he knew he was going to get better, they were going to be all right, and there was something about his tone of voice that made her believe him.

That was three years ago, and today, Mr Hall and Mrs Hall are still together and happy, and Darren and Karen are still in the house that Darren built, and they are happy as well. Darren works as a fork-lift truck driver in Bristol airport, and he takes his son to the leisure centre every Saturday morning, religiously. He's trying to teach Mervyn to swim. Karen says the boy's a bit of a daddy's boy.

They had a barbecue last week. Mr and Mrs Hall were there, Mr Prentice, and one or two others who'd helped with the building of the house. After a few drinks, Darren went up to his probation officer and said, 'You should bottle me and Karen and Mervyn, you know.'

He said, 'Why's that?'

And Darren said, smiling, 'Aren't we one of your few success stories in the probation service?'

Sometimes, in the evenings, when Mervyn's in bed, Darren'll take Karen's hand and he'll say, 'It's funny, you know, how once I wanted to be out and about and I couldn't stop tearing around, and now I couldn't be happier, being here, with you, and I don't ever want to move from this house.'

The Fate Formula

Elizabeth Arnold

'Kirsty May you're such a wimp! It'll be a great concert.'

'I have this essay to finish and . . .'

'You can study any time.' Sophie shook me, as if trying to knock in some sense. 'This is a once in a life time.'

'Not for Kirsty,' Megan said, 'she has a dad like you wouldn't believe.'

'He's out tonight, drinks with the boys, I have to catch up.' I tried to make my tone light. 'You can't study with ornaments crashing round the house like you had the wildest poltergeist in the world.'

'You don't join in anything!' Sophie sulked, and she stomped off to tell the rest of the gang that I had chickened out yet again.

The Fate Formula

'You should have accepted,' Megan warned. 'That's three invitations in a row you've refused, they'll set you a *dare*.'

My mood flipped from miserable to manic-depressive. Nobody *ever* broke a dare. They were set, like the punishments, by committee. Our crowd was the most exciting in the area, and the most dangerous. The dares were so bad they made you want to die, but not so bad you ever did . . . so far!

All day I worried. All through chemistry with Potty Pringle, who was determined we couldn't learn unless lessons were 'fun'. All through a boring English class where the only relief from prissy Miss Dempsey was the unsavoury suggestion whispered by David to Michael, and all through set prep, where I could see little notes being passed round, and little nudges and winks that meant the next victim on the gang hit list would be *me*.

I tried to slip quietly out of school the back way, but they were waiting.

'We've decided.' Michael told me. Sophie and Megan had the decency to look sheepish. David grinned.

'You're boring,' Sandra Wilson said. 'We don't like boring.'

'Potty Pringle is boring too,' Sophie chipped in, centre crowd queen as usual. I glared at her so hard she stopped smirking.

'We decided that as two negatives make a positive, you and he might . . .'

'Oh yes, what a giggle,' I said as if I believed the whole thing was a huge joke. 'I have to go home. I can't be the catalyst for World War Three.'

Michael and David gripped my arm. 'You can go,' David said, 'but here is the dare. By next Friday, Potty Pringle has to give you a proper wrap-round *hug*.'

'I can't he's . . .'

'Almost a recluse?'

'Blushes if you even look at him?'

'Boring beyond belief?'

'A dead man?'

I pretended to laugh as Megan eased us away from the gang, my gang, the crowd that had been with me since year seven. Today I hated them. 'Don't forget!' Michael shouted to our retreating backs. 'A dare is a dare. We don't want to find you naked in the swimming-pool at home time do we?'

Weekends are like living nightmares. Dad spends most of the time bashing and bawling. Mum and I try to melt into walls so as not to upset him. Friday is our one peaceful night, he *never* comes home. This Friday was different. He didn't come home but it was anything but peaceful.

'Your dad's been with his floozie again!' Mum stomped round the house. 'There's perfume on his shirt! Smell this.'

'He might stay away more,' I said hopefully.

It was the wrong thing to say. My mum flared at me. 'I've put up with the swearing, the bullying, everything. I've put up with it because at least he was *mine*. Things were very bad or very good.'

I bit my lip. I couldn't ever remember 'very good'.

'Every night this week there's been perfume. How *could* he?'

I wondered what sort of world my mother lived in. I obviously knew him better than she did. He could, he certainly could, he was known throughout town as a bit-of-nasty, so even when he wasn't home he made my life a misery.

Luckily Mum didn't need an answer, she was too busy shredding his shirts into tiny strands with a kitchen knife.

I felt free to ponder my own problems. I wished I had a shirt to shred but not even a million shirts would make me feel good. The thought of the gang dare haunted my every move, every breath. How on earth was I supposed to get a smooch from passive Paul Pringle? The nerd who only came to life when he had a test tube in one hand and a small flask in the other.

My legs are long, I've got boobs to be quite proud of. Dad once said I was pretty – 'so I want you in by ten my girl or I'll skin you' – Ten! Small wonder I can't go anywhere!

I tried to imagine a Paul Pringle cuddle. When? Where? How? I wasn't sure which was worse, the physical contact, or the idea of half the world's heads bobbing up and down as they watched through the window. The whole thing was impossible.

'I've finished the shirts,' Mum said proudly. 'Any chance of a cup of tea, Kirsty? You look a bit pale, I'm not upsetting you am I? I'm on to CDs now.'

My mother, my normally wrung-out rag-doll mother, filled a bucket with bleach and calmly started dropping CDs in, slowly, one by one.

'You better take that outside,' I said, reaching for the kettle. 'You might kill someone.'

'I'd like to,' Mum said without a hint of a smile, but to my relief she dragged the bucket out into the garden.

Dad stayed away until Sunday, it was too long. By the time he returned Mum had every single possession he owned in the hall . . . micro-chipped.

Dad opened the door, gaped at the mountain of multi-textured scraps, at my mother sitting on the stairs waiting patiently for him to explode, and last but not least at the gleaming knife that rested too quietly on her lap. He fled.

'Would you have used it?' I asked, feeling safe enough now to admit the whole thing was *not* a huge joke.

'Oh yes!' Mother said sweetly. 'But I only planned a *small* dissection.'

I expected tears, but no, we actually quite enjoyed Sunday night.

We piled all Dad's scraps into big dustbin liners and dumped them in the shed. We cleaned up, made supper and shared a giant bottle of wine.

'Aren't you sad?'

'Relieved really . . . I think. You can't live with a total wally for ever can you?'

I wanted to say, I hope not, but this was her character assassination not mine. I just shrugged.

'I'm sorry if I'm upsetting you but sometimes . . .'

'I'm *fine*,' I said, and suddenly it was true. Dad was gone, the house was peaceful, and best of all, I knew exactly how to fulfil my dare.

The smooch turned out to be the easy bit. By Monday lunch-time everyone knew that my dad had left and my mum was about as cuddly as a coiled python.

'You poor thing!' Miss Dempsey said, trying to turn into a sympathy queen. I could almost see her ticking off score points on her child psychology sheets. I wanted to shout, Don't bother I'm perfectly happy! but I didn't. I flushed with embarrassment and said, 'I have to go to my class, exams close and all that.' So now I was brave as well.

'There, there,' Miss Dempsey said, patting me as if I was her stupid poodle. 'Now if you have any problems . . .'

'Yes, yes. I must go.'

'Well don't forget, Mr Pringle is most kind . . . most kind.'

I looked worried all through class. I didn't laugh when Potty Pringle waved the iodine bottle about while he was talking and splattered it all over his shirt. I didn't laugh when Sophie had to do *six* titrations to get even close to an answer. I didn't even laugh when Miss Dempsey popped in to see how I was and spent all her time gazing at Pringle with great moo-cow eyes.

At the end of the lesson I collapsed sobbing by his desk. It wasn't difficult. I was in absolute hysterics. Exit class plus one minute, and already Michael, Sophie, Megan, Sandra and David were outside gazing in, their noses pressed expectantly against the window.

I turned away, trying to make sure Pringle wouldn't spot them. My shoulders were shaking with a curious mix of laughter and fear. I sobbed even louder. Paul Pringle rested a very nervous hand on my shoulder.

'Kirsty May . . .'

I swung round to face him. Five heads ducked down and up. I pressed my shaking body next to his and automatically his arms closed round me. Outside I heard a muffled cheer. I was bottom of the dare list . . . free again . . . only I wasn't.

I realised in that moment that something had gone terribly wrong. I discovered a new fundamental.

Wimp + Wimp = Explosion

I felt a fire light within me, a yearning that ruptured out from the heart of me. I was hot, I was cold, I was burning with need. I raised my head, and for the first time Paul Pringle and I gazed deep into each other's eyes.

'You better go,' I said huskily, knowing my every move was being watched.

'Yes, I'd better go,' Paul Pringle agreed, making no attempt to move, or to hide the rush of desire that flushed all over his face.

I pushed him gently, pretending to look for a hanky for the sake of the gang.

Paul Pringle stood looking shaken. Boring had become quiet and serious. Passive had turned to passion. I knew now that those thin arms were strong, that his lanky body was demanding. I licked my lips, unsure what to do.

'Feel better now?' Paul asked, his voice in automatic mode.

'No,' I told him truthfully, 'I feel a million times worse.'

Paul Pringle didn't laugh. He backed away but his eyes never left mine. 'So do I, Kirsty May.'

It was easy to make sure I met Paul alone. He was a creature of habit. He always walked home along East Street, turned down Roman Road, and then down a long narrow leafy lane that cut through to the Malvern Estate. We met as if by chance and nothing had changed, one look said everything.

I was glad he was shy. It was like we were both sixteen, each simple touch was electric, each word suppressed desire, each hope each fear each dream a mountain of emotion. Together we were vibrant, alone we were nothing. True love was everything I had ever dreamed it would be.

At first Mum worried I was out so much, so I said Megan needed me to help her with exam work. Megan was not impressed. 'It's *dangerous*, the dare's over, Kirsty.'

'I love him,' I told her crossly, 'and he loves me, and that's all that matters.'

'But it's not that simple. You're a schoolgirl, he's a teacher, and worse than that Miss Dempsey's got the hots for him.'

'I don't care!' I shouted, but I did, I hated Miss Dempsey for wanting him, Megan for trying to stop me loving him, and all of our gang for trying to make out it was just a bit of fun.

'I've never felt like this,' Paul told me one day as we lay side by side on the riverbank watching a kingfisher skitter over the water. 'I never believed I could be so happy.'

I thought of my dad, violent, chucked out, pseudo-repentant, back now and *still* putting my mum down. My Paul could never be like that, every word was a caress, every touch an explosion. I would love him for ever. I turned my face to his, I lost my mind with the taste of him. I wanted time to stop. I wanted to stay like this for ever.

The next day I learned that ever was over. I was loitering in the lane that backs on to the playground with Michael and David, while Sophie finished her smelly old fag. On the other side the head was talking.

'You think Mr Pringle is having an affair with Kirsty May? That's a very serious allegation, Miss Dempsey. If he is, he'll have to go, leave at once.'

'Not an *affair*!' Miss Demsey said hastily, and suddenly I was grateful that she had an eye for him. 'I just think they are growing too close, what with her father being such a nightmare. I just think we should . . .'

'My staff have a moral obligation,' the head said firmly. 'I shall ask questions. If I find there's a hint of a problem, he *goes*.'

All the blood drained from me. I felt cold and sick and oh so bitter. My legs folded, instinctively Sophie and Megan grabbed hold of my arms.

'You told them!' I accused. 'You *told* them!'

'Don't be so stupid! When has our crowd ever told tales?' David said calmly. 'It's not one of *us*.'

'You've been seen, you must have been.'

'Or someone's just sensed a different kind of chemistry: Nerd × Nerd = Nerd^2.'

'I can't have his career ruined. We'll have to be more careful,' I said hopefully.

'Fat chance! He's more love sick than you are,' Sophie snorted.

'And he'll tell the truth if asked,' Megan said. 'He's the sort of nerd that never knows when to lie.'

They were right. Paul Pringle would give up everything for me. I just could not let that happen.

I worried all through chemistry. I didn't laugh when Paul made a joke that was really funny. I didn't laugh when he waved Miss Dempsey away because he was halfway through an experiment. I didn't smile when he winked at me. I worried and worried and worried, but at the end of the lesson I had a plan.

We met at our favourite place by the river. We held hands and I wanted us to stay, peacefully side by side, for ever.

'I love you,' Paul told me, his eyes tearing pieces from my heart. 'I love you very much, Kirsty May.'

It was Megan who said the words I just could not say. She popped out of the bushes with the rest of the gang hooting with laughter.

'It was only a *dare*, Mr Pringle. We dared her.'

'She only smooched you for a bet.'

'She hates her dad, she wasn't crying for *him*!'

Paul stood up and raised me gently to my feet. 'Say it isn't true, Kirsty May.'

I said nothing. Tears streamed down my face. I could not bear to look at him.

'*Say it isn't true, Kirsty May*!'

'Sir, it's true!' Megan said desperately. 'She never loved you, it was all just a dare.'

I hated them for helping me. I hated them for helping him. I hated myself for having to be strong for both of us. I hated the world. I fled.

It's over! The emptiness grows deeper every moment. I understand now why my mother closes her eyes to things she does not wish to see.

I dare not look him in the eye. I am a robot in a time loop. My heart screams every time Miss Dempsey flashes her eyelashes, or her legs, or her hopes.

I did the right thing. The head asked everybody he could: 'Did you hear of a dare?' They all nodded. Paul Pringle is safe but I am dying inside.

Miss Dempsey is working her way through her psychology sheet on love. I could tell her everything. I could tell her she'll never ever have him. He gave his heart to me and I broke it. One day, when it's

Elizabeth Arnold

safe, I'll give it back, every single piece, and in doing so, I might have a chance of mending mine.

All for Love

Jenny Koralek

'And all for love, and nothing for reward' Edmund Spenser, *The Faerie Queene*.

First came famine and flight.

Then death.

And Naomi, whose name means sweet, became Mara, the bitter one. And in her bitterness did not believe that she would ever feel joyful again.

It had been, of course, all for love that Elimelech, Naomi's soldier husband, saddled up horses to carry her and their two sons swiftly across the river out of the starving land of Judah into the lush valleys of Moab, a land of idol worshippers, but where the harvests had not failed.

Elimelech found favour in the eyes of the Moabite king who made him captain of the palace guard and for ten years the family lived in comfort and safety. Naomi kept a good house, a fine house even, and with her beloved, handsome Elimelech watched their sons, Chilion and Mahlon, grow up.

And then Elimelech died. Struck down at sunset by a fever which carried him off before sunrise. Naomi was a pious woman. She bowed her head and murmured 'The Lord has given and the Lord has taken away. Blessed be the name of the Lord,' but for the first time in her life the words brought no consolation of any kind.

Nevertheless because she loved her sons dearly, she hid her grief and loneliness, and when they got married took their wives to her heart: pretty little Orpah and solemn, dark-eyed Ruth, daughters of the king.

But that same heart, already bruised and battered, finally broke when, within a space of seven days, both her sons died one after the other, Mahlon following Chilion into death just as he had always followed wherever he led in life.

Orpah ran to her own mother, weeping and calling upon the many gods of Moab, but Ruth stayed close to Naomi and shared her silent sorrow.

All for Love

She watched her mother-in-law pray to her mysterious, invisible one God and longed more than ever to be part of her world. Belonging to a country where every man had as many wives as he liked, Ruth had been astonished and moved to discover that her husband's love had been for her alone.

Naomi felt as if she was in a long bad dream from which there could be no awakening unless... unless... Here flickered one vital thought like a light in her dark cave, faint at first but slowly growing stronger. The thought became a voice, saying: *Go home, Naomi! It is time to go home.*

Ruth had grown to love her mother-in-law very much. Ever since her wedding day when Naomi had hugged her and drawn her into the house it had been an undreamed of, true homecoming.

She had never met a woman like her: always the first one up to see that the bread was fresh and the breakfast milk still warm from the goat; carrying food to the poor and herbs to the sick; spinning soft wool against the bitter winter snows; down in the vineyard picking the tender grapes; always busy, yet never too busy to talk with her and Orpah, or to listen to their worries and their woes and now, to let them weep in her arms.

'I'm coming with you!' Ruth said at once when Naomi found the courage to tell the girls her decision.

Jenny Koralek

'And so am I,' cried Orpah.

'No, my darlings,' said Naomi. 'You must go home now to your mothers. I have no more sons for you . . .'

'Let us at least come with you to the frontier,' begged Ruth.

'Very well,' sighed Naomi, 'but there we must part, we three lonely women. You must find new husbands who can give you children, and I must cast myself on the mercies of my own people . . .'

The three women set out.

As Ruth dragged her feet through the hot red dust of the desert road, the intense pain she felt at the thought of being parted from Naomi grew harder and harder to bear.

When they reached the frontier Naomi stopped and, turning to Ruth and Orpah, said in a firm voice, 'And now, goodbye, my dear daughters. Go home. Go home! Your father will look after you. You are both young. It is certainly not too late for you to find new happiness . . .'

She put her arms round Orpah and kissed her, gently nudging her towards the way they had come.

But Ruth did not wait for Naomi's parting embrace. She ran to her and flung her arms round her, sobbing.

'No!' she heard herself cry, like some animal in pain. 'No, Naomi, no! We have been together too long to be parted now. When I married your son *you* became my mother . . .'

Orpah stopped in her tracks. Ruth could see the turmoil flitting across her face as if she feared that perhaps she should have said something similar.

But nothing could stop Ruth now.

'I don't care what you say, Naomi!' she went on. 'Wherever you go, I go. And wherever you live, I will live. I long for your people to be my people and for your God to be my God. Where you die, I will die and there I will be buried, and I swear here and now to your God that nothing, *nothing* except death can part us now.'

Like the first rays of the sun after the long, dark night, the warmth of this unsought gift of love flowed through Naomi, washing away much of her bitter grief. And with the warmth came relief. She would not be going home alone. She would enter the gates of Bethlehem with a loving daughter at her side. She was too moved to speak, but slipped her arm through Ruth's and together they watched Orpah turn away. It was not long before they saw her wipe away her tears on her sleeve and her steps grow lighter and quicker as she disappeared into the distance.

'Dear little Orpah,' sighed Naomi. 'I hope she will be all right.'

'Of course she will,' said Ruth.

They smiled at one another and turned westwards to Bethlehem.

They were barely through the gates of the city when some women came running towards them.

Jenny Koralek

'Aren't you the wife of Captain Elimelech who went to Moab during the famine?' they asked Naomi.

Naomi wept: 'Yes, indeed. I left home a joyful wife and mother and return a sorrowing widow, who would be childless without Ruth, this dear daughter-in-law . . .'

The women sighed and murmured as Naomi told them her story and they would not leave them until they had found lodgings.

They had arrived in Bethlehem at the beginning of the barley harvest. 'We have a custom in our land,' Naomi explained to Ruth on their first night. 'The poor – and we are very poor, Ruth – may go into the fields and follow the reapers and pick up any corn they let fall.'

'I will go tomorrow,' promised Ruth.

She woke up before sunrise full of sudden doubts about whether she had been wise to leave her own country and family without so much as a backward glance.

She looked at the sleeping Naomi, who was trusting her to fetch barley for their daily bread and, somehow, found the courage to get dressed and set out for the fields, in spite of great waves of homesickness.

She was soon walking behind the reapers gleaning the corn they let fall.

Chance had led her to land which belonged to Boaz, a wealthy cousin of Naomi's husband. When he came out from Bethlehem later that day to see how the day's work was going, he saw Ruth in his field of pale-gold swaying barley. And he fell in love with her: How lovely she is, lovely to look at and lovely the way she walks so shyly and quietly behind my reapers; how gracefully she stoops to gather the fallen corn.

He strode over to his steward at once and asked him who the girl was. 'Of course, you don't know!' said the servant. 'You have been away! Naomi has returned from Moab. That young woman is her devoted daughter-in-law, Ruth, who refused to be parted from her ... left mother, father, country, everything ...'

But Boaz was already halfway across the field, trying to slow himself down as he drew closer to Ruth so as not to frighten her.

'Please!' he said breathlessly, 'don't be afraid ... this is my field ... no need to go elsewhere for your barley! I shall tell my servants to look after you and whenever you are hungry please go and help yourself to bread and figs, and when you are thirsty please go and drink from the waterpot there in the shade of the olive trees ...'

Before Boaz could stop her, Ruth had fallen to her knees, her dark eyes full of tears, murmuring words of thanks.

He drew her gently to her feet and, as her small hands touched his, a great love welled up in Ruth for Boaz. It overflowed, warm and golden, into his love for her, a new love, vibrant and harmonious as a joyful musical chord.

Jenny Koralek

But neither of them said a word.

Before he left the field Boaz gave orders to his servants to let Ruth take barley even from the sheaves, which made the servants smile to themselves and murmur, 'Our master must be in love to allow that!'

'Someone has been very generous!' exclaimed Naomi when Ruth came home that evening with pink cheeks and a full load of corn in her apron.

'God bless the good man who let you work in his field. Who was he?'

'Boaz,' said Ruth dreamily. 'His name was Boaz.'

'*Boaz*?' cried Naomi. 'Why, he is a relative, a cousin through my marriage to Elimelech, *and* a widower! Oh, Ruth! We now have a protector!'

'He says I can take corn from the sheaves and come every day till the harvest is over,' said Ruth.

He's in love with her, said Naomi to herself. And she with him . . . He's bound to marry her when all the corn is in! 'God bless the man,' she said aloud.

But when all the grain had been gathered in and Boaz had not said anything about marriage to Ruth, Naomi decided to take matters into her own hands.

'I would not be a good mother-in-law,' she said to Ruth one night,

All for Love

'if I did not wish to see you once more happily married. Now, listen: Boaz, as a close relative of both your husband and mine has the right to marry you. This is a law from the time of Moses to stop land from going out of the family . . . I can't think why he has not yet spoken of it. Well, tonight he will go down to the barn to keep an eye on the threshing. So, I want you to wash and perfume yourself and put on clean clothes and go down there, but not before he has had his supper and gone to sleep. Then I want you to go in and lie down at his feet. And don't be afraid: we already know he is a gentle and good man. He will understand what this means and will make you his bride.'

Ruth trusted Naomi completely, so she did as she was told and when it was dark, crept into the barn and lay down at the feet of the sleeping Boaz.

In the middle of the night Boaz was woken by a dream and found Ruth lying there.

'Oh my beloved girl!' he whispered. 'I dreamed of you! I dreamed that you became my bride and that the cherubim and seraphim flew about us murmuring that we would have a son whose son would be the father of a great king, a giant-killer, a maker and singer of psalms, who in turn would be father to the wisest king the world has ever known or will ever know . . .'

Boaz covered Ruth's hair, her face, her hands with tender kisses, murmuring, 'Oh, beloved girl! I want to marry you more than anything

Jenny Koralek

in the world! But I am afraid I am too old for you! And for days I have been tortured by the knowledge that I have an older brother who, by law, has more right to you than I have . . .'

'We must trust in your God,' said Ruth, 'that your dream will come true.'

They lay quietly in each other's arms till just before dawn when Ruth slipped away unseen and hurried home to tell Naomi everything that had happened.

'Be patient,' smiled Naomi. 'Boaz will find a way to marry you before the day is out.'

Boaz rose at sunrise and went in search of his brother, Tob, and to his astonishment met Tob coming to find him.

'I had a dream last night!' said Tob. 'A dream that I was being made to marry a Moabite girl to redeem some land that belonged to her dead husband here in Bethlehem!'

'It is true,' sighed Boaz with a heavy heart. And he told his brother the story of Naomi and of Ruth, the devoted daughter-in-law.

'So, you see,' he concluded. 'It is your duty to marry her.'

'But I can't marry her!' said Tob. 'I can't! I won't marry a girl who does not come from the land of Judah! A foreigner! A heathen! A worshipper of idols! Yes, yes, you can tell me till the cows come home that she wants to follow our God and our ways. But it never works. No, brother! I'm sorry. *You* will have to marry her!'

All for Love

So Boaz married Ruth and before the next barley harvest Naomi was sitting at the door in the cool of the evening holding their son. Her broken heart was healed and the dream that Boaz had told Ruth that night in the barn did come true. From this line woven entirely from love came great kings: the brave David, the wise Solomon, his son, and also, some believe, the carpenter Joseph, father of Jesus Christ.

EDITED BY MIRIAM HODGSON

Love Hurts

In this superb collection of twenty-four stories, love is portrayed in all its many guises with realism and humour.

Featuring stories by Vivien Alcock, Annie Dalton, Marjorie Darke, Berlie Doherty, Adèle Geras, Mary Hooper, Monica Hughes, Mollie Hunter, Pete Johnson, David Johnstone, Geraldine Kaye, Jenny Koralek, Anthony Masters, Jenny Nimmo, Michael Pearson, Joan Phipson, Ann Pilling, Alison Prince, Dyan Sheldon, Ian Strachan, Jean Ure and Diana Wynne Jones, with a foreword by K M Peyton, winner of the Carnegie Medal.

A bumper collection of stories previously available in three volumes – *The Teens Book of Love Stories*, *Heartache* and *Take Your Knee Off My Heart*.

EDITED BY MIRIAM HODGSON

In Between

First kisses, standing up for other people and making decisions on one's own. Eleven funny, sad and brave stories about growing-up, reflecting the moment when childhood is left behind.

The prize-winning and best-selling contributors are: Vivien Alcock, Rachel Anderson, Joanna Carey, Adèle Geras, Elizabeth Laird, Sam McBratney, Michael Morpurgo, Alick Rowe, Ian Strachan, Robert Westall and Jacqueline Wilson.

'An excellent collection . . . A must . . .'
School Librarian

'. . . strong, involving stories.'
Junior Bookshelf